Before July 2012, who could have predicted that Psy would become Korea's most famous pop star?

debut each year. From 1998 until 2008, about thirty K-pop groups, duos and solo artists were introduced each year. In 2009, the number leapt to more than forty. Then nearly seventy in 2010. And more than a hundred in 2012. Clearly, no book can cover all of K-pop but I hope this book will include most of your favorites.

So, what does it all mean? Aside from Psy, the top K-pop acts often get ten million to thirty million hits for their videos, with the biggest songs topping fifty million views,

and Girls' Generation's "Gee" now over one hundred million. A hot new song from a big star can rocket to the top of the iTunes charts all over the world, at least for a day or two after it gets released. Western music websites like Popdust regularly feature articles about Korean music, and when Korean artists face off against the biggest American pop stars in online polls, the Korean artists usually win hands down. K-pop may not be dominating sales but its fans are numerous

enough and passionate enough to make a real difference.

K-pop may not get much play on Western radio or much respect from "serious" journalists but that's mostly a sign of how the middle-aged powers that be often just don't get it. But the stars of K-pop—along with the songwriters and producers and fans—know what they like.

People have been underestimating K-pop since the music started. They won't be underestimating it anymore.

CHAPTER 1 | THE LAND

The sun rising over Seoul as the nation's capital wakes up in the morning.

THE LAND OF K-POP

Gangnam Intersection is the heart of Seoul's richest business district, the part of town made famous in Psy's "Gangnam Style."

You can't really understand K-pop without knowing something about the land that gave rise to it. It's no surprise that modern Korea is as flashy and exciting as the music it has created. Just as K-pop continually changes and moves forward, in Korea change is the only constant, especially in Seoul.

There was a time not long ago when Seoul was overwhelmingly drab, full of boring concrete and ugly buildings. Not anymore. Today's Seoul looks to dazzle with amazing shops, the coolest styles, and more and more incredible modern architecture. Walking around the fancy shops by Dosan Park or the winding streets of Hongdae, you quickly understand how the dazzling world of K-pop was born here.

Seoul is the biggest city in Korea, home to ten million people, with another ten million living in the suburbs and surrounding cities. It's huge. And although Seoul is more than 600 years old, most of the city is actually quite new. After the Korean War (1950–3) pretty much leveled everything, there were barely one million people living there. But as Korea recovered from the war, the country rebuilt, and Seoul in particular rebuilt like crazy, re-fashioning itself again and again.

Today, Korea and its capital Seoul are barely recognizable compared to what they were a generation ago. If you want to know what K-pop is really about, you have to understand where it came from. You need to walk the meandering alleys of Samcheong-dong, close to the ancient Gyeong-bokgung Palace in the heart of the city. You need to see the brightly lit bridges that cross the Han River.

Today, there are four main neighborhoods if you want to know the cool Seoul: Hongdae, Samcheong, Gangnam and Apgujeong. A city the size of Seoul is, of course, full of interesting and amazing areas but these are key.

Hongdae—"Hongdae" being short for Hongik University in Korean—is the main artsy area in Seoul, home to the most popular nightlife area for university students, young artists and indie music. It's also the headquarters

of YG Entertainment, one of the "big three" music labels, which owns big hip-hop clubs like NB as well as restaurants and other buildings right in the heart of the neighborhood.

Located in western Seoul, in an area rich with top universities, this part of town has long been a bit different. Back when most of Seoul shut down at midnight, Hongdae clubs kept the music going all night long. Artists flocked here for weirdness and cheap rent

Gwanghwamun is the front gate to Seoul's most famous palace, Gyeongbokgung, first built in 1395.

(although it's not cheap anymore). The first techno clubs sprang up here, and today there are dozens of live music clubs and hundreds of bars and other cool hangouts. A weekend flea market in the park at the heart of Hongdae brought in young people selling cute handmade wares of all sorts, further shaping the character.

It is also home to the Coffee Prince café where the famous TV drama of the same name was shot. There are several theaters in the neighborhood, including the strange curvy building that houses a special theater just for Nanta, a leading Korean performance

group (Nanta has four specialized theaters around Seoul). The famous punk brand Bratson also calls Hongdae home, although its main store is across town in the Hannam-dong neighborhood. Bratson is a major staple of YG Entertainment's stars, so if you want to buy some of the wild things G-Dragon or Sandara wear in their videos, this is the place to check. There are also several huge new high-rise apartments that many K-pop stars call home, although don't expect to walk in and say "Hi." Security is tight. Besides, they are probably all out working hard somewhere.

Another great part of Seoul, located north of the Han River just to the east of the old Gyeongbok-gung Palace, is a winding, old-style area in the center of town called Samcheong-dong. When the Korean capital moved to Seoul 600 years ago, this was one of the first neighborhoods to grow up around the old palace. Over the past decade, more and more interesting shops and restaurants have moved into Samcheong-dong, making this old community one of the hippest in Seoul and a common locale for many a TV drama. Samcheong-dong, along with the nearby

Geunjeongjeon was the throne room for the Korean kings long ago.

The peaceful coffee shops of Samcheong-dong have some of the prettiest views of old Korean *hanok* homes.

SM Entertainment's headquarters in Cheongdam-dong is getting a giant facelift.

Anguk-dong and Insa-dong areas, is home to many little art galleries and artsy shops, as well as funky tea houses, restaurants, Buddhist temples and a lively street culture. Samcheong-dong is also an area rich in traditional Korean houses, or *hanok*, many of them converted into art galleries and other cafés. And if that's not enough, it is also the neighborhood where Lee Young-ae, one of Korea's top actresses, has opened a small boutique, Lya Nature, to sell organic and chemical-free children's clothes and other items.

South of the mighty Han River is where Seoul gets much more posh. Thanks to Psy, everyone now has heard of Gangnam. Gangnam may just literally mean "south of

Garosu-gil has become one of the most popular places in Seoul to rest and relax.

It's also full of shopping.

the river," but for Koreans it conjures up all sorts of ideas of modern living and luxury. A brief scene from *The Bourne Legacy* was even filmed on a back street here. But the area around Gangnam subway station is much more businesslike these days. It is the home of Samsung's massive headquarters and is a major hub for financial and tech companies.

For fashion, style and coolness, you need to travel closer to the Han River, to the uber trendy Apgujeong or, to be more specific, the neighborhoods of Sinsa, Apgujeong and Cheongdam. One of the coolest strips in today's Korea is Garosu-gil, literally "tree-lined street," a narrow kilometer-long road that cuts through Sinsa, which is full of art galleries, shops, huge coffee houses and restaurants. It's a

relatively quiet street for such a popular place in such a big city.

This is also home to one of Se7en's spicy chicken stew restaurants, Yeolbong Jjimdak, featuring plenty of pictures of the singer and his friends. Yeolbong Jjimdak is located on the south side of Garosu-gil, just off the main road.

Further up the road is the flagship location of Helianthus, one of Korea's most luxurious handbag brands. And if fancy handbags are your thing, you can check out the Simone Handbag Museum while in Garosu-gil, a ten-story building that's built in the shape of a handbag.

Just down the street from Garosu-gil, in the heart of the Apgujeong area, is Dosan Park, home to some of the fanciest shops in Korea. How fancy is it?

Well, there's a huge Maison Hermes here, just the fourth in the world, a gorgeous glass-walled building that seriously impresses. It's also the home of actor Bae Yong-joon's Gorilla in the Kitchen restaurant, a healthy themed restaurant that uses no oil or creams. There's also an extremely funky Ann Demeulemeester shop that's completely covered in greenery; the building was designed by Mass Studies, one of Korea's most creative architecture firms. The luxury lifestyle brand Man Made WooYoungMi is also located in Apgujeong, along with many other super fancy shops.

After Apgujeong comes the Cheongdam-dong district, which is even posher. This area is the home to many music labels, including SM Entertainment, JYP Entertainment and Cube Entertainment.

The Galleria department store in Apgujeong has long been one of the fanciest places to shop in Seoul.

Across the street from SM Entertainment is Korea's very own 10 Corso Como, and in the alley behind SM is Jung Saem Mool, one of Korea's best beauty salons. Jung Saem Mool is very pricey, but its hair and makeup artists regularly work with many of Korea's top stars. For a more artsy shopping experience, you can try Daily Projects, which features plenty of books on design and art in a great space.

The sidewalks outside of all three major music labels are popular places for fans to camp out, hoping to catch a glimpse of their favorite stars, but the area around JYP Entertainment is especially popular. Located in a small alley off the main road, with Cube Entertainment just a few

meters away (and, best of all, a donut shop across the street, to help you kill time), this unassuming strip can get especially full in good weather.

Incidentally, if you are looking to pick up the latest K-pop gear, Cube has a Cube café full of shirts, CDs and other goods, while across town at the famous Lotte Department Store, SM Entertainment has been opening a temporary "pop-up" shop during the big tourism seasons in January and the summer where you can pick up goods by your favorite bands.

For all my talk of fancy shops and upscale brands, even the poshest parts of Seoul can be surprisingly mixed, broken up by old Internet cafés or donut shops. That's always been a defining part of Korea, the mix—combining new and old, fancy and simple, loud

and quiet, cutting edge and retro. Koreans call it *jjamppong*, "all mixed up." Usually used to refer to a spicy seafood soup, *jjamppong* has long seemed like the most Korean of words to me.

Despite Korea's unceasing push toward the future, there are still hints and tastes of its cool past that linger. A palace here. An old neighborhood there. Korea and Seoul have reinvented themselves so many times already over the past few decades, and those reinventions lay beside each other, overlapping and layering, creating the country it is today. It's hard to imagine, but for most of Seoul's history it existed only on the north side of the Han River. Today, it sprawls in all directions, forever growing higher, faster, flashier. And it is that mix of elements that has also created K-pop.

K-POP?

The Wonder Girls' biggest hit, "Nobody," featured a retro 1960s style.

WHAT IS K-POP?

If Korean music fans' biggest question was when would K-pop break out in the West, in the West the biggest question has probably been "So what is K-pop anyway?" K-pop literally means "Korean pop," as in pop music, but of course the term stands for much more than that.

At first glance, the beats and dancing and videos look familiar, much like a variation of American pop music. But the closer you look and the more you listen, the more differences you notice. Like when I heard a K-pop song in a Barcelona café, I could identify something different about it even before I heard the singers' language. There is something distinct and special about K-pop. It's like everything is a little bit louder, the images brighter, the style flashier—it's just *more*.

Ever since the modern pop music industry began a century ago, it has been international, from the jazz of the 1920s to the rise of rock 'n roll to disco to the hundreds of types of music we have today. Much of the time, that has meant musical ideas arising in the United States and traveling to the world—but not always. The British Invasion, which brought the Beatles and the Rolling Stones to the United States, is probably the most famous example. Bossa nova, Brazil's samba-influenced jazz that became very popular in the 1950s and 1960s, is a favorite of mine. Scandinavia has its heavy metal. And, today, Korea has K-pop.

So where did K-pop come from? Although the hip, exciting Seoul of today is rather new, it's worth remembering that Koreans have long been a very musical people. Chinese diplomats returning home hundreds of years ago commented on how much Koreans love to sing. Even Korean traditional music

CAPTURING THEIR FAVORITE IDOLS

was unique in East Asia for its focus on free-form, almost jazz-like improvisation and reinterpretation. Western music came to Korea in the late nineteenth century, bringing new scales and instruments, and jazz was quite popular in the 1920s.

In the aftermath of the Korean War of 1950–3, both sides of the divided peninsula were devastated, but soon Korea's strong-willed, dynamic people began rebuilding their country. By the 1960s, South Korea was undergoing an artistic renaissance, and one of the most exciting aspects of that era was its music. Rock, folk and funk all flourished in the late 1960s and early 1970s as young people became caught up in the excitement of an all-new era. Sadly, though, this era would not last. South Korea's government was quite authoritarian at the time and none too fond of the counter-culture elements of the day, so it cracked down hard in 1975. Many of Korea's top musicians were sent to jail or drummed out of the music industry, leaving a very different music scene behind. Tastes also changed, and by the 1980s rock was much less popular, leaving ballads and plenty of cheesy synthesizers and syrupy pop music (not to mention oodles of oversized shoulder pads).

Through all these changes, Korea continued to transform. Its economy surged and expanded at an amazing rate. The military government came to an end in 1987, and the new constitution that came into being allowed greater freedom of expression and restored democracy. The Seoul Olympics of 1988 were a symbol of how much the country had grown and opened up. And thanks to the growth of the economy and freedom, Korean arts and entertainment were soon recovering.

BTOB IS A YOUNG GROUP BUT IT ALREADY HAS MANY FANS

There was popular music before K-pop, of course. Cho Yong-pil was one of the biggest artists of the 1980s, although he faded in the early 1990s before making a spectacular and totally unexpected comeback in 2013 with "Bounce," a song that dethroned Psy from the top of the charts. Kim Kwang-suk was an important and influential folk singer, closely associated with the democracy movement. Sinawe was probably the biggest heavy metal group ever, peaking in the late 1980s and early 1990s. Kim Gun-mo was huge for much of the 1990s, although his more jazzy, grown-up pop songs never really fitted the K-pop mold. Shin Seung-hoon was the biggest ballad singer of the early 1990s, back when ballads ruled the charts. But none of these acts were K-pop, at least not the K-pop we would recognize.

The rise of modern K-pop couldn't be clearer. It began on March 23, 1992, the day that Seo Taiji and the Boys released their first album. Seo Taiji (born Jung Hyun-chul) had dropped out of school at seventeen and briefly played with Sinawe before hooking up with b-boy dancers Yang Hyun-suk and Lee Juno. They formed a hip-hop group heavily influenced by New Jack Swing, but also a jumble of musical

MISS A MEETS WITH FANS

ideas, and featured plenty of energetic dance moves. Most older Koreans were confused by this new musical concoction, but young people loved it. "Nan Arayo" ("I Know") spent most of the year on the top of the charts, starting a music revolution.

Seo Taiji was not the only one dreaming of new musical styles, of course. Another producer trying to figure out the new sounds of a new generation was Soo-Man Lee. Lee had been a popular singer,

CUBE STUDIO

deejay and television host in the 1970s before leaving Korea to study electrical engineering in California. While he was studying engineering, he was also studying MTV and the biggest trends in American music, and working out how to bring these trends to Korea. Soon after returning home, Lee started SM Entertainment. He tried making stars of several promising young talents but was not quite able to find the magic formula.

Not until he created H.O.T, that is. With H.O.T—short for "Hi-five Of Teenagers"—Lee combined the energy of new American pop music with a rigorous training system designed to create young stars. Lee realized that stars needed to learn more than just singing and dancing. They needed a whole range of skills, such as humility, attitude, language and the ability to deal with the media. H.O.T exploded on the scene in 1996, selling in huge numbers and whipping young fans into a passionate frenzy. Soon came more bands, such as the girl group S.E.S., Shinhwa and Fly to the Sky.

Lee was not alone. Yang Hyun-suk, one of the members of Seo Taiji and the Boys, started YG Entertainment in 1996. Daesung Enterprise (today's DSP) had groups like FinKL and Sechs Kies. Park Jin-young launched his solo career in 1994, then started his own music label, JYP Entertainment, in 1997. With each new group, each new producer, K-pop was growing, becoming brighter and better.

G.NA

It is important to remember that these trends and successes in music were not happening in a bubble. Korean movies, too, were ever more creative and celebrated, setting box office records and winning awards around the world. Musical theater boomed also, and today the live options are almost endless. In the arts, design, fashion and more, young talented Koreans were rewriting the notions of what Korea is and what it could do. And as each field grew, it would influence and fertilize the others, transforming the whole of Korean society.

With the turn of the new millennium, K-pop continued to grow. Korea quickly installed one of the world's best broadband Internet networks, which, while amazing for gaming and transforming day-to-day life in Korea, also meant that the Korean music industry bottomed out. Young people simply stopped buying music. Music stores disappeared. If they were to survive, Korea's music labels would have to look at other ways of making money. Some pushed their artists into commercials and acting. Others focused more on international sales. Japan, being the world's second biggest music market, was the obvious target, and SM

Entertainment's BoA was a prime example of doing great there. But many singers increasingly found fame around Asia, thanks in no small part to acting in popular TV dramas. Rain, who starred in the very popular *Full House*, is a great example of this trend. And China, although still a tiny music market, was growing rapidly, and Korea's music leaders had their eye on it. This is where the term *hallyu* came from, coined by Chinese journalists to describe the popularity of Korean artists there. Called *hanliu* in Chinese and *hanryu* in Japanese (it's all the same character, 韓流), *hallyu* literally means "Korean wave" or "flow," and soon Korean music was washing over all of Asia.

FANS HANGING OUT AT CUBE STUDIO

But the wave didn't stop there. As with Korean movies and TV shows, its music kept finding new fans. In the old days, you had to convince radio programmers or music television executives to play your music if you wanted people to discover your group. Not in the Internet age. Thanks to YouTube and other online services, fans were able to find anything they wanted and could spread the word. And the word kept spreading. If you are reading this book now, it's probably because the word spread to you as well.

JYP ENTERTAINMENT

Today, SM Entertainment, YG Entertainment and JYP Entertainment are commonly called the "big three" music labels (with Cube, which was founded by a former JYP president, often considered a

2PM

YG ENTERTAINMENT

strong fourth). Each has a pretty distinct style of music and way of doing business. SM is easily the biggest company and concentrates on more bubbly, younger pop. Having consistently produced many of the biggest groups in K-pop for nearly two decades, it can be argued that SM is the industry leader and most aware of what the fans want. Except that SM might argue it doesn't produce K-pop. It produces SM-pop—a style of its very own.

JYP Entertainment has a more R&B flavor and is strongly influenced by its founder, JY Park (Park Jin-young). Park is the main songwriter for his company's groups and the creative force. His mottos of leadership, humility and responsibility hang prominently on the walls of the JYP headquarters. He also has a long history of success, having been a big solo artist himself for many years and having worked with many of Korea's top stars. JYP used to be home to Rain, one of the biggest

K-pop stars of the last decade, and his group Wonder Girls were the first K-pop group to land on the *Billboard* charts.

YG Entertainment was founded by Yang Hyun-suk after Seo Taiji and the Boys broke up. From the beginning, YG featured hip-hop and favored attitude over the usual K-pop cuteness. But since YG struck gold with the idol groups Big Bang and 2NE1, it has pushed swag and flair to ever greater heights. YG is also home to a little solo artist by the name of Psy; maybe you've heard of him.

But there are dozens of smaller labels, too, all following roughly the same formula: recruit potential stars young, then train, train, train them incredibly hard, and put together the most promising recruits in a multi-member (and

BIG BANG

15&

nearly always unisex) band. Almost everything is done in-house, from production to publicity.

So that is some history and background about K-pop. But it still leaves the core question unanswered: What *is* K-pop? There are very few signs of traditional Korean pentatonic music in it, or of Korean traditional instruments. Increasingly, top K-pop labels buy music from international producers (and some K-pop songwriters write for Western acts, too). Detractors, even Korean ones, often accuse K-pop of not being Korean at all. But if you listen to it seriously, there is definitely something different about K-pop that stands out.

It has certainly changed a great deal from the days of Seo Taiji and H.O.T. Tinny New Jack Swing is long gone, replaced with much more of an electronic dance sound, even dub step on some songs these days, most notably on CL's "The Baddest Female." There are still a few tinges of trot here and there, but much less than there once was. A popular trend at the moment is to create songs that almost sound like mash-ups of three or four different songs stuck together at random. Although this mishmash sounds weird to many ears, it's a hyperactive style that has long been popular in Korean discos, where you often get just minute segments of a song before the deejay quickly moves on to something else. Apparently, even pop songs are not fast enough for the high-speed pace of young Korean people today.

Perhaps one of the most defining parts of K-pop is simply the language. Korean is a snappy, popping language, full of densely packed, tight syllables. In many ways, it is already halfway to hip-hop. Writing melodies for the Korean language forces the songs to reflect the language, often with more syllables

FANS GATHER TO GLIMPSE THEIR IDOLS

in a line than you'd hear in other languages. And since dance and live performances are such an important part of K-pop, songs are also written with their choreography in mind. The things K-pop sings about are different, too. There is much less storytelling than in Western music and more of a focus on describing a feeling or metaphor. While there is plenty of longing and suggestion, K-pop is usually much less graphic and sexual than Western pop (well, except for JY Park).

Perhaps most importantly, K-pop is overwhelmingly genuine. It is not a music of cynicism. When a singer loves, he loves completely. When he misses his love, it is a deep, soul-crushing ache. And most of the time, it's just fun. Sure, it can seem a little silly, even childish, but plenty of people appreciate the opportunity to forget about being cool and have a little fun.

If you have dreams of becoming a star yourself, there is good news as K-pop has gone global, and so has the search for new talent. And with new stars like 2PM's Thai-American Nichkhun, Miss A's Fei and Jia and SM Entertainment's large and growing line-up of ethnic Chinese stars, K-pop is more open to the world than ever. Even non-Asians are increasingly getting chances at stardom now, with girl group The Gloss featuring Olivia, a French woman, and Nicole Curry appearing on the audition program *Kpop Stars 2*.

2PM

However, it's still an incredibly tough slog. There are untold thousands, even tens of thousands, of young people fighting with all they've got to secure one of the few precious slots that open each year in Korea's leading music labels to become a young trainee. Of the few that make it, fewer will actually get a shot, and fewer still will make it to the big time. Between that audition and becoming a star, a trainee is in for years of brutally tough training. Not to mention that they had better learn Korean fast and well.

Step one, of course, is the audition. These days, all the big music labels in K-pop recognize the importance of finding stars, so there are more opportunities than ever to try out for a precious slot. Many, like YG Entertainment, accept online applications any time, inviting the most promising young people to live auditions several times a year. The big labels typically have one or two auditions in the United States each year, and another in Japan, and auditions in Canada, Australia, China and other parts of the world are growing more common, but of course there are more chances in Korea.

BROWN EYED GIRLS

What are the music producers and labels looking for? It's more than just a great voice. It's more than just dance moves. It's more than just a pretty face. Everyone is hungry to find *stars*—that magical but oh so elusive charisma that inspires fans. And you had better be pretty young. It takes years to create a K-pop star, more than four on average, so the window of opportunity is fairly small.

Once you pass the audition, now the hard work really starts—the training. Expect to face years of arduous work, improving your singing, dancing, languages and, most importantly, how to be a *star*. Expect long, long days, often going well into the night. Expect to sweat. Often labels expect you to live on-site, at small dormitories close to the main studio with many other aspiring young talents. It can be a fiercely competitive environment. "Cut-throat," said Jay Park in *Spin* magazine.

School, however, is usually optional. Some labels, like JYP, insist their stars do well in school and encourage their talents to get into university. Others, however, leave such decisions up to the individual.

As for dating, don't expect much. Both during training and after making their debut, artists are usually too busy to have much time to date. And, generally, music labels don't want their stars to be tied down. Idols are presented to fans as a kind of virtual boyfriend and girlfriend, so relationships ruin the illusion, not to mention that overly enthusiastic fans have been known to go crazy on girls seen dating their favorite male stars.

With such a long, relentless process to craft a star, it's difficult and expensive for the music labels. Dorms, food, classes, transportation, clothes and everything else adds up quickly, and it's been estimated that training costs the music companies around $100,000 per student each year. With K-pop groups comprising so many members and taking so many years to train, it's no surprise the management companies want to sign their recruits to such long contracts—as long as thirteen years and some even longer—and take such a large cut of the revenues. But some court cases and bad publicity have gradually chipped away at the worst types of long-term contracts. The truth is, once a performer becomes a star, the balance of power completely changes.

Television is also changing how K-pop stars are made, thanks to the popularity of *American Idol*-style audition programs. With artists like Lee Hi, Park Jimin, Busker Busker and Akdong Musicians rising to fame from TV, there's a new business model coming to K-pop with the potential to change K-pop yet again, but so far it's too early to know for sure.

One bit of more serious advice. With so many K-pop groups being formed, almost every day, not all the producers and managers out there are completely trustworthy, as is true about the entertainment business anywhere. So before you sign anything or agree to anything, make sure you've done your homework and selected carefully, and stick with people who have a well-established track record and a good reputation.

K-pop, like so much else about Korea, is constantly growing and changing. Whatever K-pop is, you can be sure that in a few years it will be something else. That is what makes K-pop so perplexing sometimes, but it is also what gives K-pop its power.

WONDER GIRLS

Eat Your Kimchi

Simon and Martina Stawski's *Eat Your Kimchi* is one of the most surprising success stories to spring from K-pop, or at least the neighborhood of K-pop. A newly married couple from Toronto, Canada, Simon and Martina came to Korea in 2008 to teach English in a Seoul suburb. To help sooth their families' worries, they started making fun little videos about their lives in Korea. But soon they grew more ambitious and began covering other subjects, including K-pop, reviewing videos and interviewing groups.

Those videos gradually caught on and now *Eat Your Kimchi* is a genuine phenomenon, with 340,000 subscribers to their YouTube channels and more than 130 million views of their videos. When Simon and Martina turned to crowd sourcing to fund a professional studio in autumn 2012, they were shocked to discover dedicated fans donated the $40,000 they needed in less than seven hours, eventually pledging more than $100,000. "We've been crying just about all day," they wrote on their website when it happened. "Wait: OK—started crying again."

K-Pop Now: How did *Eat Your Kimchi* get started?
Simon and Martina (they answered the questions together): It was just a hobby at the beginning. At first,

Simon and Martina, the couple behind *Eat Your Kimchi*, have become incredibly popular video bloggers, in part because of their regular reports on the world of K-pop.

our audience was our immediate families in Canada. We were surprised when we got our first subscriber on YouTube, and thought to ourselves "wtf? Why is someone subscribing to us?"

I think that's when we started to think seriously about the possibility of other people using our videos, so we started to create basic videos for those viewers, like how to use your T-Card. We remembered the shortage of videos on Korea at the time we came here, and figured that we just wanted to help out with things like that.

KPN: And how did your videos become a big deal?
S&M: We still find it hard to believe that something big is going on. It still doesn't really feel that way to us, you know.

Around the time that we started thinking of doing this full-time, we looked into the idea of producing regularly scheduled shows. "Music Monday" was the first show that we started, but since then we've made shows for almost every day of the week.

As for the point where our videos really took off, we can't really say for sure. We didn't have any big boom. We just steadily, very steadily grew. There was no viral video that brought in thousands of new people to the site and videos. We just, month by month, got more subscribers and viewers. That's all. It was only at the two-year mark that we saw that we could possibly grow big enough, if we continued at our rate, to grow to the point of independence, you might say. Our site's almost five years old now, and it's really been only in the last year or so that things have started to really take off.

KPN: Did you have any training in programming or media?
S&M: We're both totally untrained in programming. We have no formal education in it whatsoever. We just fiddle around with buttons until the screen does what we want it to do. We're just very inquisitive and diligent, that's all. Our video editor now is formally trained, and she keeps on using fancy pants terms and we're always looking at her confused, and say stuff like "Oh! You mean the fadoodlydoo button? Yeah that's a good button."

KPN: You've started getting huge reactions from fans, like you were K-pop stars. How did that happen?
S&M: I think we were the most shocked last year when we went to the Google MBC concert, and after the concert we got swarmed by fans. It took us 45 minutes to leave when the walk would normally have taken two minutes. Seeing so many people, in real life, outside of the Internet, was really when we started saying to ourselves, "OK, something weird's happening here...."

Just this Monday [May 20, 2013], when we arrived in Singapore, we had a very big crowd of people waiting for us at the airport, so big, in fact, that the police were called. That surprised the hell out of us, because that's usually reserved for K-pop groups.

For us, we were so happy to see so many people and we wanted to talk with everyone, not scoot off and be anti-social.

KPN: How important was K-pop in building your popularity?
S&M: K-pop really helped get us out there, though it's not our only thing. We do indie videos, travel videos, blogging, eating, etc., but our K-pop vids are where we're at our funniest. The source material is just so easy to work with! So, since we're more outgoing in those cases, and they're more shareable, then we can see that we got popular that way.

KPN: Who are your favorite K-pop groups these days?
S&M: We really like the big acts from YG: Big Bang, 2NE1 and Psy, but we also like SHINee, Super Junior, U-Kiss, T-ara and Orange Caramel.

> [... WHEN WE STARTED SAYING TO OURSELVES, "OK, SOMETHING WEIRD'S HAPPENING HERE...."]

INTERVIEW WITH
Kevin Kim from Ze:A

Kevin Kim was born in Korea but lived in Australia for many years. But his homeland called, and after passing his auditions for Star Empire Entertainment, he soon found himself in the new K-pop group Ze:A and then the subgroup Ze:A Five. When he's not singing and dancing with his groups, Kevin has acted in the musical *Love Song of Gwanghwamun*. He also hosts the Arirang Radio program *Hot Beat*, and stars in too many commercials to list. He was kind enough to talk to me briefly about becoming a K-pop idol.

KPN: What made a teenager growing up in Australia want to audition for K-pop?
Kevin: I became interested in K-pop when I was a teenager because there was the Korean wave in Australia.

My first audition was an acting audition for Martin Bedford Agency, which had famous actors such as Russell Crowe and Olivia Newton John. It was a valuable experience leaning how to act well like those people. For my K-pop audition, which was just my second ever audition, it brought me to Star Empire Entertainment.

KPN: What was the most unexpected part of the training?
I went through tough times with vocal and dance training because I was not flexible. Plus, understanding Korean culture and speaking honorific Korean were really difficult for me.

KPN: What was your first public performance like?
My first public performance with Ze:A was in Cheongju, the capital city of North Chungcheong province. We walked all over town promoting ourselves, putting up posters and talking to people. We also performed from the back of a truck, called a "wing car" in Korean. We did the wing car stunt for Ze:A fifty times all over South Korea. We just kept practicing and practicing, trying to improve our performance. We stayed up all night preparing to perform on that truck before every event, practicing and keeping each other's spirits up.

Before getting on stage the first time, I was really nervous, but as time goes by I've gotten more confident and have developed myself, step by step.

KPN: What do you most want to do artistically and musically in the future with Ze:A?
All the members of Ze:A have developed themselves in several ways, as composers, actors, emcees and singers. I helped write the lyrics for one song, "Step by Step," on our new album *Illusion*. I really want to be famous worldwide, like Michael Jackson, someone who I really admired, in the future.

Ze:A member Kevin Kim wants to be as famous worldwide as Michael Jackson was.

INTERVIEW WITH
Brian Joo from Fly to the Sky

Brian Joo and Hwanhee were part of one of the most popular K-pop groups of the early 2000s, Fly to the Sky. Although an SM Entertainment group, it was a bit unusual: it comprised a duo instead of a large group and they sang more ballads and light pop instead of electronica. After leaving SM Entertainment in 2004, Fly to the Sky continued for several years, with both Brian and Hwanhee releasing solo albums. Today, Brian continues to sing and entertain as well as host a radio show and much more.

KPN: How did you get involved in K-pop?

Brian Joo: I've wanted to be in the entertainment business since I was four years old but I really didn't see myself going anywhere with entertainment in the United States while I was growing up there. Back then, the US wasn't ready for an Asian musician, nor was it accepted. Even today, Psy has had one big hit in the US, but he's not continually coming out with stateside music. So, when I had the opportunity to audition for a Korean record label, I didn't want to lose my chance to at least try and see how far I could go.

My audition was pretty out of the ordinary. I didn't actually sign up myself, but a friend saw a flyer and contacted the casting director and pretty much got the audition booked for me. I had no idea this friend had signed me up and she had no idea that I would be contacted, but I was and it all fell into place from there. And this was back in 1997.

The process was pretty much a typical audition, I guess. They wanted to get me on film singing, dancing, acting and speaking Korean, because they needed to know how well I spoke the language, seeing that I'm from the United States.

KPN: What was most different about the process compared to what you expected? What was hardest? The most fun?

Brian: I had no thoughts beforehand as I had nothing to compare the process with. I pretty much did as I was asked and it was a nerve-wrecking experience because I was only sixteen years old at the time. The fun part of it was when the casting director called me back and told me that a big-time record label wanted to see me in person and that they would cover all expenses for me to fly to Korea and back. I just thought to myself, if I don't get picked or signed up, then at least I'll get a paid vacation!

KPN: If you could change one thing about the Korean music business, what would it be?

The one thing I would change would be artistic freedom. I know a few musicians do what they want,

"THE ONE THING I WOULD CHANGE WOULD BE ARTISTIC FREEDOM.... THE MAJORITY ARE LIKE PUPPETS."

but the majority are like puppets. Record labels make them perform the songs that they feel are right and they dress the boy bands and girl groups the way they feel fit. I feel that more freedom should be given to artists in Korea.

KPN: Looking at K-pop today, what do you see as the biggest difference from when you first broke into the business?
Well, the biggest difference is that people from *all* over the world listen to K-pop and actually love the music. Back when I started, the Internet wasn't so advanced and people didn't realize what K-pop was. Back then, K-pop wasn't called K-pop, it was called Gayo.

KPN: You are now very involved in CrossFit. How did you get involved in this? What is so special about it?
Brian: Well, I was always into fitness, but never found a way of working out that I really liked. Then a friend introduced me to CrossFit and I got deeply involved in it. The main reason I enjoy it is because it's a challenge every time I do a CrossFit workout. And I see myself getting better day by day, so it's definitely a healthy addiction that I don't want to stop.

Brian Joo, as a member of Fly to the Sky, played a key role in the early days of K-pop.

CHAPTER 3 | BOY GROUPS

BIG BANG

YG Entertainment

MEMBERS
T.O.P (Choi Seung-hyun; 최승현) November 4, 1987
Taeyang (Dong Young-bae; 동영배) May 18, 1988
G-Dragon (Kwon Ji-yong; 권지용) August 18, 1988 (leader)
Daesung (Kang Dae-sung; 강대성) April 26, 1989
Seungri (Lee Seung-hyun; 이승현) December 12, 1990

KOREAN ALBUMS
Since 2007 (2006)
Remember (2008)

KOREAN MINI-ALBUMS
Always (2007)
Hot Issue (2007)
Stand Up (2008)
Tonight (2011)
Alive (2012)

JAPANESE ALBUMS
Number 1 (2008)
Big Bang (2009)
Big Bang 2 (2011)
Alive (2012)

SOLO ALBUMS
T.O.P
GD & TOP (2010)
Taeyang
Hot (2008)
Solar (2010)
G-Dragon
Heartbreaker (2009)
GD & TOP (2010)
One of a Kind (2012)
Coup d'Etat (2013)
Daesung
D'scover (2013)
Seungri
VVIP (2011)

FAN CLUB VIP
OFFICIAL COLORS Black and
  yellow

Big Bang in a performance
on *M! Countdown* in 2012.

In addition to its envelope-pushing music, Big Bang is known for its outrageous fashion.

If K-pop turns everything up to eleven, Big Bang goes to twelve. Even by the flashy standards of K-pop, Big Bang is a little wilder, a little crazier. Big Bang "gets its crayon," as G-Dragon (Kwon Ji-yong) would say.

Since its 2007 debut, Big Bang has made a name for itself as one of the most dynamic groups in K-pop, throwing together an incredible variety of sounds and visual styles, often within the same song. With two rappers in the group—G-Dragon and T.O.P—who have quite different styles and are able to rap melodiously, Big Bang is also unusually versatile. From the beginning, the guys of Big Bang have been heavily involved in shaping their own sound and writing their own music, making their music distinctly their own.

If ever someone was raised to be a star, it must have been G-Dragon. Having performed in the group Little Roora since he

G-Dragon

Daesung

Taeyang

T.O.P

Seungri

was just seven years old, G-Dragon trained for years at SM Entertainment before finally finding a home at YG Entertainment. Since making his debut with Big Bang, G-Dragon has shown a flair for the wild, wearing an ever-changing array of over-the-top outfits. His solo work has proven immensely popular also, with several Western music critics citing "Crayon" as one of the top songs of 2012.

In September 2013, G-Dragon released his second full-length album. *Coup d'Etat* unsurprisingly shot to the top of all the charts both in Korea and abroad, earning plenty of raves for its typical envelope-pushing style. G-Dragon rapped with Missy Elliot on "Niliria," rocked in London on "Crooked," and just got strange in the video for "Who You?" He even got a little tender on the ballad "Black" with Jennie Kim singing along.

Like G-Dragon, Taeyang joined YG when he was eleven, and together the two can be seen in the old Jinusean video for "A-Yo." Originally, the two of them were going to be a duo, before the record label changed its mind and decided to put together a larger group.

T.O.P spent his early teenage years rapping under the name Tempo before getting picked by YG. In addition to performing with Big Bang and solo, T.O.P has been the most successful actor in the group, playing roles in movies like *71: Into the Fire* and TV shows, such as the hit *Iris*.

Daesung is Big Bang's main vocalist and is confident enough that he even released a "trot" single—usually music you think of for older people and miles away from Big Bang's usual hip style.

Seungri hails from Gwangju, where he used to be a member of a dance team (Korea has some of the world's best breakdance teams). Although YG originally cut Seungri from the group during a reality program that highlighted the creation of Big Bang, Seungri was given a second chance and this time he made the cut.

The bad boys of K-pop, Big Bang has weathered a few scandals over the years. But for their dedicated fans, a little naughtiness only makes their bang even bigger.

In 2012 and 2013, Big Bang's world tour took them to twelve countries, where they played for 800,000 fans. Between the tour and all their solo projects, it was hard to believe that it was more than a year without a new release by one of the biggest groups in K-pop. YG Entertainment has promised more is on the way, but for Big Bang's dedicated fans, "later" is too far off and "more" is never enough.

Big Bang beat some stiff competition on the March 15, 2012 episode of Mnet's *M! Countdown* thanks to its super hit "Fantastic Baby."

SUPER JUNIOR

SM Entertainment

Super Junior became one of the biggest groups in K-pop by becoming, literally, one of the largest groups in K-pop. Since making its debut in 2005, Super Junior has wowed audiences all over Asia, topping the charts in China, the Philippines, Taiwan and Thailand. The group has even been depicted on Chinese postage stamps!

From the beginning, Super Junior was created with an eye on the international market. For its subgroup Super Junior-M, ZhouMi is Chinese and Henry is Taiwanese-Canadian, and just a couple of months after Super Junior's first single was released, it was topping the charts in Thailand. Its first album in 2005 did well, and *Don't Don*, released in 2007, was even bigger, but Super Junior's third full album, *Sorry, Sorry*, was

MEMBERS

LeeTeuk (박정수) July 1, 1983 (leader)
HeeChul (김희철) July 10, 1983
YeSung (김종운) August 24, 1984
KangIn (김영운) January 17, 1985
ShinDong (신동희) September 28, 1985
SungMin (이성민) January 1, 1986
EunHyuk (이혁재) April 4, 1986
DongHae (이동해) October 15, 1986
SiWon (최시원) February 10, 1987
RyeoWook (김려욱) June 21, 1987
KyuHyun (조규현) February 3, 1988

SUPER JUNIOR-M MEMBERS

ZhouMi April 19, 1986
Henry October 11, 1989

KOREAN ALBUMS

SuperJunior05 (Twins) (2005)
Don't Don (2007)
Sorry, Sorry (2009)
Bonamana (2010)
Mr. Simple (2011)
Sexy, Free & Single (2012)

KOREAN MINI-ALBUMS

Show Me Your Love (2005) (featuring TVXQ!)
U (2006)

JAPANESE SINGLES

Bonamana (2011)
Mr. Simple (2011)
Opera (2012)
Sexy, Free & Single (2012)
Hero (2013)

FAN CLUB ELF (Ever-lasting Friends)
OFFICIAL COLOR Pearl sapphire blue

Super Junior is one of the largest boy bands in K-pop.

arguably its biggest, becoming a massive success all over Asia.

Then the hits kept coming. In fact, in Taiwan Super Junior ruled the No. 1 spot on the KKBox online music chart for Korean singles for 121 straight weeks, going from "Bonamana" to "Mr. Simple" to "Sexy Free & Single" without a break.

Sub-units were a key part of Super Junior from almost the very beginning, with Super Junior-K.R.Y. (consisting of KyuHyun, RyeoWook and YeSung) releasing its first single in late 2006, and Super Junior-T (for "trot" music) making its debut in early 2007. Super Junior-M (as in "Mandarin") is for Chinese-language songs. Super Junior-H (for "happy") features LeeTeuk, EunHyuk, KangIn, ShinDong, SungMin and YeSung, and the

duo DongHae and EunHyuk.

Today, Super Junior has more than 6.5 million "likes" on Facebook and each member has huge followings on Twitter—from 600,000 all the way to 3.5 million for DongHae and 3.8 million for SiWon. Plus millions more on China's Weibo, Korea's Cyworld and other social media sites. And they're still getting bigger. Their latest world tour, "Super Show 5,"

Although they started out as boys, today the Super Junior members have grown into men.

has taken the group all over the world, with twenty-seven shows in fifteen countries. Playing to tens of thousands of fans at a time, Super Junior's latest three-plus hour concert has won raves for being one of the biggest and best K-pop shows ever put on. "Pure, unadulterated, and spectacular entertainment," raved one newspaper in the Philippines.

With so many members, it is no surprise that Super Junior has continued to evolve. Several of the members are currently fulfilling their military service requirement, leaving about eight active members in the group. But if anything is clear about Super Junior, it's that many more hits are on the way.

ShinDong

Kangln

SungM

TVXQ!

SM Entertainment

TVXQ! may mean "Rising Gods of the East," but in fact this group has already ruled the top of the K-pop charts for the better part of a decade.

MEMBERS
U-Know (정윤호) February 6, 1986
MAX (심창민) February 18, 1988

KOREAN ALBUMS
Tri-angle (2004)
Rising Sun (2005)
«O»-Jung.Ban.Hap. (2006)
Mirotic (2008)
Keep Your Head Down (2011)
Catch Me (2012)

KOREAN MINI-ALBUMS
Hug (2004)
The Way U Are (2004)
Christmas Gift from Dong Bang Shin Gi (2004)
2005 Summer (2004)

JAPANESE ALBUMS
Heart, Mind and Soul (2006)
Five in the Black (2007)
T (2008)
The Secret Code (2009)
Tone (2011)
Time (2013)

FAN CLUBS Cassiopeia (Korea), Big East (Japan)
OFFICIAL COLOR Pearl red

MAX and U-know, the guys behind one of the biggest groups in K-pop, TVXQ!

The name TVXQ! is based on a four-character phrase that works in Korean, Chinese and Japanese, but it sounds completely different in each language. 東方神起 is Dong Bang Shin Ki in Korean but Tong Vfang Xien Qi in Chinese and Tohoshinki in Japanese.

Founded in 2004, TVXQ! soon became one of SM's greatest successes, with a pop sound that featured plenty of a cappella and simple piano melodies. But the band took its fame to a whole new level in 2006 with its album *Mirotic*, which was nothing less than one

of the defining albums of K-pop; the electronic dance song "Mirotic" is a true classic. And like many K-pop groups, as their careers developed, the duo became more active in writing and producing their own songs. But perhaps their biggest legacy is their international

popularity. For people who became K-pop fans in the mid to late 2000s, TVXQ! was the group they identified with. And this was no accident. SM Entertainment formed TVXQ! specifically with overseas markets in mind. They first created a huge following in Japan, but soon Thailand, China and the rest of the world followed.

Today, U-Know and MAX are going stronger than ever. Their latest international tour, which went to China, Malaysia, the United States, Chile and elsewhere, sold out in record time. Their 2013 Japan tour filled five giant stadiums for multiple shows, bringing in a record-setting 850,000 fans. And their latest

Japanese single, "Ocean," is selling as big as any TVXQ! hit.

Having just turned a decade old since their debut in December 2003, TVXQ! is definitely one of the defining groups of K-pop. No longer boys, U-Know and MAX are now young men at the top of their game. There's no limit to how far and how high TVXQ! might go.

MAX and U-Know are constantly showing off different and fresh styles in TVXQ!, from the young and playful to the grown-up and formal.

2AM

Big Hit Entertainment

2AM and 2PM will forever be linked as both groups originally presented as an eleven-man group called One Day, as profiled in a reality TV documentary, *Hot Blood*. But One

Day was a bit of a trick, as JYP Entertainment founder JY Park actually intended to form two bands, one for more up-tempo dance music—2PM, of course—and one focusing on ballads and more emotive songs—2AM.

Despite having just four members, 2AM as a group is surprisingly diverse. Changmin is a rare K-pop star who performed his military service before joining the music label. He's also one of

the fastest recruits to go from signing up to debut, joining 2AM just three months after signing with JYP.

That's a big contrast to Jo Kwon, who trained for nearly seven years. Even though he was in training for so long and was the last member chosen for 2AM, he became leader of the soulful singing group. Today, Kwon is in big demand as a variety star (he joined the cast of *We Got Married* in 2009, *Family Outing* and

Seulong, Changmin, Jo Kwon and Jinwoon form one of the quieter groups in K-pop, yet their fans still scream plenty loud.

many other shows). He is also a TV actor and now a musical actor, having starred in a Korean production of *Jesus Christ Superstar*.

Jinwoon is a K-pop star with rock roots, having played in a band in high school. Even today, he is known to play guitar as well as some light rock, and has performed solo at a couple of music festivals.

Seulong has a diverse and interesting selection of side

2AM at the 2010 edition of the Golden Disc Awards in Seoul, where they won the digital grand prize.

MEMBERS
Changmin (Lee Changmin; 이창민) May 1, 1986
Seulong (Im Seulong; 임슬옹) May 11, 1987
Jo Kwon (Jo Kwon; 조권) August 28, 1989 (leader)
Jinwoon (Jeong Jinwoon; 정진운) May 2, 1991

KOREAN ALBUMS
Saint O'Clock (2010)
One Spring Day (2013)

KOREAN MINI-ALBUMS
Can't Let You Go Even If I Die (2010)
F. Scott Fitzgerald's Way of Love (2012)

JAPANESE ALBUM
Voice (2013)

FAN CLUB IAM
OFFICIAL COLOR Metallic gray

projects. He acted in the TV series *Dream High* and the movie *26 Years*, based on the famous Kang Full web comic. And he recorded a Korean cover of "Levels," the huge techno hit by Avicii.

2AM might also be the tallest band in K-pop, with three of the four members topping 180 cm.

2PM

JYP Entertainment

MEMBERS
Jun. K (ex-Junsu) (Kim Min-jun; 김민준) January 15, 1988
Nichkhun (Nichkhun Buck Horvejkul; 닉쿤) June 24, 1988
Taecyeon (Ok Taec-yeon; 옥택연) December 27, 1988
Wooyoung (Jang Woo-young; 장우영) April 30, 1989
Junho (Lee Jun-ho; 이준호) January 25, 1990
Chansung (Hwang Chan-sung; 황찬성) February 11, 1990

PAST MEMBER
Jay Park

KOREAN ALBUMS
The First Album 1:59PM (2009)
Hands Up (2011)
Grown (2013)

JAPANESE ALBUMS
Republic of 2PM (2011)
Legend of 2PM (2013)

JAPANESE MINI-ALBUM
Still 2:00PM (2010)

FAN CLUB Hottest
OFFICIAL COLOR
Metallic gray

The up-tempo half of almost-group One Day, 2PM is the flagship guy group for JYP Entertainment. Soon after the *Hot Blood* documentary that introduced 2PM and 2AM, 2PM spilled onto the K-pop scene in 2008 with "10 Out of 10," a high-energy, rock-guitar dance song and a video that featured a lot of impressively athletic dance moves. But it was their next single, "Again and Again," with its catchy, beeping hook, that turned the band into true superstars.

It's been a tough climb for the young stars, though, after they were forced to re-tool on the fly just a year after their debut, after losing their high-profile leader Jay Park in 2009. But thanks to the dedication and hard work of these six idols, 2PM has become one of the biggest groups in K-pop.

One of the most notable differences of 2PM is Thai-American member Nichkhun, one of the first non-Koreans to be featured in a K-pop group. Nichkhun was scouted by JY Park at a K-pop event in America when he was a teenager, then brought over to Korea for training. Fluent in

2PM getting ready for a big show.

Thai, Nichkhun has become a leading idol for K-pop's international spread, especially in Thailand, of course, but throughout the region as well.

It's also worth noting that Chansung, the youngest member of 2PM, was one of the most successful artists before the band was ever formed, having acted in

Taecyeon, Jun. K, Chansung, Junho, Wooyoung and Nichkhun in action.

the popular comedy *High Kick!* in 2006.

Compared to most K-pop groups, 2PM has gone with a look that's a bit more mature and grown-up, although that style seems to have caught on recently and more groups are sporting suits and ties these days. Also unusual for K-pop, 2PM has no "leader."

Since Jay Park left the group, they've decided that they don't need anyone to claim the captain's chair, opting instead for a more equal arrangement.

After taking a two-year hiatus (that's like a generation in K-pop terms) to concentrate on overseas promotions, 2PM returned with a well-reviewed comeback, *Grown*.

Despite having one of the best songs in the group's history (the elegant and sophisticated "A.D.T.O.Y."), the singles on *Grown* did not set the night on fire, but album and concert ticket sales have been as huge as ever, showing that the future is shining bright for one of Korea's most exciting acts.

B.A.P.

TS Entertainment

MEMBERS
Yongguk (Bang Yong-guk, aka Bang and Jepp Blackman; 방용국) March 31, 1990 (leader)
Zelo (Choi Jun-hong; 최준홍) October 15, 1996
Jong Up (Moon Jong-up; 문종업) February 6, 1995
Youngjae (Yoo Young-jae; 유영재) January 24, 1994
Daehyun (Jung Dae-hyun; 정대현) June 28, 1993
Himchan (Kim Him-chang; 김힘찬) April 19, 1990

KOREAN MINI-ALBUMS
No Mercy (2012)
One Shot (2013)

KOREAN SINGLES
Warrior (2012)
Power (2012)
Stop It (2012)

FAN CLUB Babies
OFFICIAL COLOR n/a

B.A.P. may be a new group, having released its first single in 2012, but it is clear about its ambitions. Just take a look at the name. B.A.P. stands for Best Absolute Perfect. With a name like that, you'd better be able to walk the walk. But considering all the best new band awards it won in 2012, it looks like B.A.P. is going to be walking for some time.

Compared to much of K-pop, B.A.P. tries for a tougher, dirtier style, with stronger hip-hop elements. Leader Youngguk used to be known as Jepp Blackman when he got started in the indie hip-hop group Soul Connection. He also writes many of his own lyrics, going back to his pre-B.A.P. days, helping shape the group's sound.

Himchan, although also a rapper, has a much more unusual background, having gone to the National Korean Traditional Music Junior High and High School. Even now, he continues to study performing arts at the Korea National University of Arts.

The video for B.A.P.'s single "One Shot" most definitely featured

B.A.P. won plenty of rookie awards when it made its debut in 2012.

many, many more shots than one, and is a wonderful example of the Korean saying "You die, I die." Everybody dies. Given that "One Shot" shot to the No. 1 spot on *Billboard*'s World Music chart, though, B.A.P. obviously knows what it's doing.

Despite being such a new band, B.A.P. has already had a solo tour of the United States, playing in four cities in 2013. Most unusual for a K-pop group, it played in the US before trying out Japan, usually the first place groups go to outside of Korea.

B.A.P. performing at Arirang TV's *Wave K* in 2012.

BEAST

Cube Entertainment

Usually written as B2ST because "2" is pronounced "ee" in Sino-Korean, Beast has grown incredibly popular since its debut in 2009. But it is a bit of an unusual group, considered by many to be a band of cast-offs, filled with members who were cut from other music labels. Leader Doojoon, for example, had been on the reality TV program *Hot Blood*, which introduced 2AM and 2PM, but was one of the unfortunate guys who didn't make the cut. Hyunseung just missed the cut for Big Bang.

Fortunately, Cube Entertainment saw the potential in this potent sixsome, and, thanks to some creative songwriting and production by Shinsadong Tiger, one of Korea's leading music makers, Beast has become a beast on the charts. Its music is some of the fastest in K-pop, with unbeatable and cutting-edge production.

While all the members of Beast contribute to their albums, Junhyung is by far the most active, with credits on dozens of their songs, both for the lyrics and songwriting; in fact, he's one of the most prolific songwriters in K-pop today, trailing only G-Dragon and Shinhwa's Min-woo.

MEMBERS
Doojoon (Yoon Doo-joon; 윤두준) July 4, 1989 (leader)
Hyunseung (Jang Hyun-seung; 장현승) September 3, 1989
Junhyung (Yong Jun-hyung; 용준형) December 19, 1989
Yoseob (Yang Yo-seob; 양요섭) January 5, 1990
Gikwang (Lee Gi-kwang; 이기광) March 30, 1990
Dongwoon (Son Dong-woon; 손동운) June 6, 1991

KOREAN ALBUMS
Fiction and Fact (2011)
Hard to Love, How to Love (2013)

KOREAN MINI-ALBUMS
Beast Is the B2ST (2009)
Shock of the New Era (2010)
Mastermind (2010)
My Story (2010)
Lights Go On Again (2010)
Midnight Sun (2012)

JAPANESE ALBUM
So Beast (2011)

FAN CLUB B2UTY
OFFICIAL COLOR Dark gray

With a string of big hits, the six members of Beast, from left Junhyung, Doojoon, Yoseob, Gikwang, Dongwoon and Hyunseung, have proven that they are nobody's cast-offs.

Despite having been K-pop stars for four years now, Beast has only released one full album in Korea and one in Japan, preferring instead to focus on EPs or mini-albums. But given the huge successes those mini-albums have had, you cannot argue with the strategy. In fact, it looks like it is the future for K-pop.

Beast has been lighting up the skies around the world with a flurry of big concerts outside of Korea. Together with other Cube artists, Beast had the first paid-ticket K-pop concert in South America in 2011. Their 2012 tour took them to eight countries, including Germany, Thailand and Indonesia, and 2013 saw them performing in Malaysia.

BUSKER BUSKER

Chunchung Music

If I were to tell you about a Korean music artist who came out of nowhere in 2012, using social media and word of mouth to become the biggest star of the year, you'd probably think I was talking about Psy. But in Korea, another band became a hit just as surprisingly and accidentally as Psy did—Busker Busker.

The guys in Busker Busker are accidental stars. The band began as an informal busking group playing on the streets of Cheonan, about an hour south of Seoul. Band leader Jang Beom-jun got the idea of trying out for the audition program *Superstar K3*, mostly because he hoped a brief bit of exposure on TV would raise the band's profile enough that local merchants would let them play around their stores. He never expected his band would get on.

The producers of *Superstar K3* also never expected the band to catch on. But catch on Busker Busker did. Big time. *Superstar K3*'s audience loved the quirky band of folk rockers, and despite the best efforts of the producers, Busker Busker kept winning. In the end, the group came second, losing to Ulala Session, but there was no doubting that the real winner with the public was Busker Busker, whose debut album was one of the biggest sellers of 2012.

Busker Busker, a trio that writes and plays its own music, is one of the biggest surprises in Korean music.

Kim Hyung-tae, Jang Beom-jun and Brad Moore are as surprised as anyone that they have become pop stars.

Despite some attempts to turn Busker Busker into K-pop stars, the band has remained true to its own music. Unlike most K-pop bands, its audience is a bit older, as the band is particularly popular on university campuses around Korea, where its members get mobbed by fans as enthusiastically as anything put out by the big three labels.

Busker Busker had yet one more big surprise in store. In spring 2013, a year after its first album came out and eight months after

MEMBERS
Jang Beom-jun (장범준) May 16, 1989 (leader)
Kim Hyung-tae (김형태) December 21, 1991
Brad Moore August 3, 1984

KOREAN ALBUMS
Busker Busker 1st Album (2012)
Busker Busker 2nd Album (2013)

the band stopped promoting it, Busker Busker suddenly returned to the top of the Korean music charts. No one really knows why. Perhaps the warm weather of spring made people think of

Busker Busker's fresh, spring-like music.

The group's second album, which was released in September 2013, is a mellower, sadder collection of songs than the first, but it rocketed to the top of all the charts just the same. While the first album had a strong spring vibe, Jang said he considers the second to be more of an autumnal evening. Regardless, Busker Busker is proof that music stardom comes in many different shapes and sizes in Korea.

CN BLUE

FNC Entertainment

CN Blue has one of the more
unusual origin stories in the world
of K-pop. Instead of being put
together by a music management
company in Korea, the members
started out playing in small clubs
and on the streets of Japan. With
little money or support, and less
than stellar Japanese skills, their
record label sent them to Japan in
early 2009, trying to create a buzz

MEMBERS
Jung Yong-hwa [정용화] June 22, 1989
Lee Jong-hyun [이종현] May 15, 1990
Kang Min-hyuk [강민혁] June 28, 1991
Lee Jung-shin [이정신] September 15, 1991

PAST MEMBER
Kwon Kwang-jin [권광진]

KOREAN ALBUM
First Step (2011)

KOREAN MINI-ALBUMS
Bluetory (2010)
Bluelove (2010)
Ear Fun (2012)
Re:Blue (2013)

JAPANESE ALBUMS
Studio albums
Thank U (2010)
392 (2011)
Code Name Blue (2012)

JAPANESE MINI-ALBUMS
Now or Never (2009)
Voice (2009)
Lady (2013)

FAN CLUB Boice
OFFICIAL COLOR Blue

CN Blue got started
in Japan before
becoming popular in
Korea and elsewhere
in Asia.

by playing live. Later that year, they released their first mini-album in Japan. With its English-only songs, it did not do particularly well, A second mini-album in November also didn't sell much. But it was a start. That autumn, FNC Entertainment got Yong-hwa cast in the TV drama *You're Beautiful,* along with FT Island's Lee Hong-ki, and this greatly raising his profile.

In January 2010, when CN Blue finally released its first Korean mini-album, led by the single "I'm a Loner," the band found itself on the path to stardom.

CN Blue has one of the more convoluted names in K-pop. "CN" stands for "code name," while "Blue" is supposed to be an acronym for the guys' characters:

Lee Jong-hyun got B for "burning," Kang Min-hyuk L for "lovely," Lee Jung-shin U for "untouchable," and Jung Yong-hwa E for "emotional."

As CN Blue's career has developed, the guys have gotten more involved in the songwriting, helping further create a more distinctive sound for the group. By the time of its first full album, *First Steps*, CN Blue had a hand in the writing of all the songs.

Lee Jung-shin, Jung Yong-hwa, Kang Min-hyuk and Lee Jong-hyun playing on *M! Countdown* in April 2012.

Being one of the few K-pop groups whose members play their own instruments when they play live, CN Blue is unusual in the world of K-pop. The group once opened for Linkin Park in Japan— something it would be hard to imagine another K-pop group doing—and now that it's touring beyond Asia, to the United States, the UK, Australia, and beyond, the world will soon know what the fuss is all about.

EXO

SM Entertainment

With an all-Korean team and a second group for the Chinese market, could EXO be the future of K-pop?

Soo-Man Lee, the founder of SM Entertainment, set his sights set on China from the earliest days of his music empire. And while many SM acts have had a lot of success in the Middle Kingdom, Lee took his ambitions to the next level with EXO, the first truly Korea–China joint project. More than just a group with a couple of Chinese members in it, EXO boasts two full line-ups: EXO-K for Korea and EXO-M for China.

The group's first two singles, released in early 2012, mostly just introduced the band, but with its next song, "MAMA," released in both Korean and Chinese versions, EXO rocketed up the charts in both Korea and China.

With fan bases established in both countries, EXO released *XOXO (Kiss & Hug)*, its first full-length album in June 2013, and it instantly shot up to No. 1 on all the Korean charts, led by the catchy hit "Wolf." The album came in two versions, "Hug" in Chinese and "Kiss" in Korean. A combined version hit No. 1 on *Billboard*'s World Music chart and No. 23 on its Heatseeker album chart. *XOXO (Kiss & Hug)* has sold more than 930,000 copies, something that no album has done in Korea since 2001.

MEMBERS
EXO-K
SuHo (김준면) May 22, 1991
BaekHyun (변백현) May 6, 1992
ChanYeol (박찬열) November 27, 1992
D.O. (도경수) January 12, 1993
Kai (김종인) January 14, 1994
SeHun (오세훈) April 12, 1994

EXO-M
Kris November 6, 1990 (leader)
Xiumin (김민석) March 26, 1990
Lu Han (루한) April 20, 1990
Lay (레이) October 7, 1991
Chen (김종대) September 21, 1992
Tao (타오) May 2, 1993

KOREAN ALBUM
XOXO (Kiss & Hug) (2013)

KOREAN MINI-ALBUM
MAMA (2012)

FT ISLAND

FNC Entertainment

FT Island surprised Korea's pop scene when it made its debut in 2007 with the single "Love Sick," which topped the charts for two months, followed by the album *Cheerful Sensibility*, the sixth biggest seller for the year.

With Choi Jong-hoon on guitar and keyboards, Lee Hong-ki on vocals, Lee Jae-jin on bass, Choi Min-hwan on drums and Song Seung-hyun also playing guitar and singing, FT Island was one of the rare K-pop groups to play instruments and sound more like a rock band. At first, FT Island played several shows in the Hongdae part of Seoul, the indie music center of Korea, to build up its popularity. By 2008 it was already traveling overseas, first to Malaysia and Thailand and then to Japan, Singapore, Taiwan and elsewhere.

After Lee Hong-ki got sick and hurt his vocal chords in late 2008, the music label created a three-man version of the group that came to be called FT Triple. Even after Hong-ki got better, he and Seung-hyun were in such demand for acting and hosting other television programs that the subgroup was needed to fulfill

hungry fans' expectations. In FT Triple, the three guys mix up their roles a bit, with Jae-jin switching to guitar and vocals and Jong-hoon playing the keyboards, while Min-hwan continues on drums.

As cool as it may sound to find audiences overseas and get to travel to them, it is not without its risks. In 2009, while filming a music video in Cebu in the Philippines, a typhoon struck, stranding the band there for several days.

MEMBERS
Choi Jong-hoon (최종훈) March 7, 1990
Lee Hong-ki (이홍기) March 2, 1990
Lee Jae-jin (이재진) December 17, 1991
Choi Min-hwan (최민환) November 11, 1992
Song Seung-hyung (송승현) August 21, 1992

PAST MEMBER
Oh Won-bin

SUBGROUP
FT Triple

KOREAN ALBUMS
Cheerful Sensibility (2007)
Colorful Sensibility (2008)
Cross & Change (2009)
Five Treasure Box (2012)

KOREAN MINI-ALBUMS
Jump Up (2009)
Beautiful Journey (2010)
Return (2011)
Memory in F.T. Island (2011)
Grown-Up (2012)

JAPANESE ALBUMS
So Long, Au Revoir (2009)
Five Treasure Island (2011)
20 (Twenty) (2012)
Rated-FT (2013)

JAPANESE MINI-ALBUM
Prologue of F.T. Island: Soyogi (2008)

FAN CLUB Primadonnas
OFFICIAL COLOR Yellow

For seven years, FT Island has been delighting fans all over Asia.

Song Seung-hyung,
Lee Hong-ki and
Lee Jae-jin on stage
at JTBC's *Music on
Top* in March 2012.

INFINITE

Woollim Entertainment

Infinite was created in 2010 by Tablo and Mithra from Korea's pioneering hip-hop group Epik High (in fact, L and Infinite first appeared in the music video for Epik High's "Run"), but the group's first mini-album, *First Invasion*, released the same year, met with an underwhelming response.

Its next EP, *Evolution*, which came out in early 2012, did a little better, with Infinite's "scorpion" dance for the song "Before the Dawn" gaining a lot of notice. It was finally the single "Be Mine" from its first album, *Over the Top*, that led Infinite to stardom, winning it its first weekly music program.

But it was the group's single "The Chaser," released in 2012, that took Infinite to the top of the K-pop ranks. "The Chaser" was a true phenomenon, holding the No. 1 spot on the Korean charts for weeks. *Billboard* called it the top K-pop song of 2012.

Group leader Sungkyu released a solo record, "Another Me," in 2012, with more of a rock style than Infinite's, teaming up with Nell, one of Korea's few mainstream rock acts. Then, in early 2013, Infinite launched its first subgroup, the hip-hop styled Infinite-H. Featuring

Infinite was put together by Tablo and Mithra from the famous hip-hop group Epik High.

Infinite playing at its first concert in February 2012.

band members Dongwoo and Hoya, Infinite-H topped the charts, thanks to collaborations with some of Korea's top producers, including Zion-T, Beenzino and Primary.

As Infinite has grown more popular, its overseas fan base has surged. Its "One Great Step" tour, that kicked off in Seoul in August 2013, was one of the most ambitious ever in K-pop history, especially for such a young group. The tour will consist of thirty-one shows in four legs, with concerts all over Asia, North America, South America and Europe.

MEMBERS
Sungkyu (Kim Sung-kyu; 김성규) April 28, 1989 (leader)
Dongwoo (Jang Dong-woo; 장동우) November 22, 1990
Woohyun (Nam Woo-hyun; 남우현) February 8, 1991
Hoya (Lee Ho-won; 이호원) March 28, 1991
Sungyeol (Lee Sung-yeol; 이성열) August 27, 1991
L (Kim Myung-soo; 김명수) March 13, 1992
Sungjong (Lee Sung-jong; 이성종) September 3, 1993

SUBGROUP
Infinite-H

KOREAN ALBUMS
Over the Top (2011)

KOREAN MINI-ALBUMS
First Invasion (2010)
Evolution (2011)
Infinitize (2012)
New Challenge (2013)

KOREAN SINGLES
Inspirit (2011)

JAPANESE ALBUMS
Koi ni Ochiru Toki (2013)

JAPANESE SINGLES
«BTD (Before the Dawn)» (2011)
«Be Mine» (2012)
«She›s Back» (2012)

FAN CLUB Inspirit
OFFICIAL COLOR Pearl metal gold

MEMBERS
Thunder (Park Sang-hyun; 박상현) October 7, 1990
Mir (Bang Chyul-yong; 방철용) March 10, 1991
Seungho (Yang Seung-ho; 양승호) October 16, 1987
G.O. (Jung Byung-hee; 정병회) November 6, 1987
Lee Joon (Lee Chang-sun; 이창선) February 7, 1988

KOREAN ALBUMS
Blaq Style (2011)
Smoky Girl (2013)

KOREAN MINI-ALBUMS
Just Blaq (2009)
Y (2010)
Mona Lisa (2011)
100% Ver. (2012)

JAPANESE ALBUM
Blaq Memories (2012)

FAN CLUB: A+
OFFICIAL COLOR Pearl chocolate

MBLAQ

J-Tune Camp

Rain was the biggest star in K-pop in 2007 when he broke away from JYP Entertainment and started his own music label, J-Tune Entertainment (and J. Tune Camp). Rather than just be a one-man show, Rain set to work training his own K-pop band. Two years later, MBLAQ made its debut at a major Rain concert, providing the band the kind of start that most other bands would kill for.

While all five MBLAQ members are solid singers and dancers,

Thunder probably gets most attention because of his older sister, singer Sandara Park (Dara) of 2NE1. After living in the Philippines for several years, where she gained fame as a singer, Dara moved to Korea with Sang-hyun when she joined YG Entertainment. Sang-hyun tried out at a few different entertainment companies before catching Rain's attention, where he was reborn as Thunder for the K-pop group MBLAQ.

While Lee Joon is also notable for his role with Rain in Rain's Hollywood martial arts movie *Ninja Assassin*, in which he played a younger version of Rain's character Raizo, for MBLAQ's fans, all five guys are equally awesome.

As MBLAQ caught on, its popularity spread not just around Asia but also to the West, with songs like "This Is War" and "Mona Lisa" turning up on charts in Germany and Bulgaria.

But in this writer's opinion, MBLAQ's most interesting song was its 2013 comeback song, "Smoky Girl." With a more grown-up look to the band in the music video, "Smoky Girl" also featured production by leading Korean team Primary, Simon D and Zion T, all from the exciting indie hip-hop label Amoeba Culture. A smooth and sophisticated combination of different elements, "Smoky Girl" was one of the smartest pop songs of the year.

MBLAQ was originally put together by K-pop icon Rain, but today it's a force unto itself.

MBLAQ has a reputation for having some of the best dancers in K-pop.

SHINee had one of its best years in 2013, thanks to hits like "Dream Girl" and "Why So Serious?"

SHINEE

SM Entertainment

Formed in 2008, SHINee is yet another SM Entertainment success story. The group started out strong, thanks to *Replay* and *The SHINee World*, beating out such big names as U-Kiss and 2PM to win the top newcomer award at that year's Mnet Asian Music Awards. But it was *Year of Us* in 2009 with its crazy popular single "Ring Ding Dong" that caused SHINee to really take off to K-pop super stardom.

SHINee is probably SM's most physically fit group. The group members' impressive array of bulging muscles and chiseled abs is well highlighted in their exceptional dance moves. *Billboard* magazine praised their choreography in the "Everybody" music video as some of the best of 2013. At the same time, the guys project a soft, slightly androgynous look, with plenty of long, well-moussed hair.

SHINee, comprising from left ONew, JongHyun, Key, MinHo and TaeMin, has been one of the biggest music award winners since the group's debut in 2008.

MEMBERS
ONew (이진기) December 14, 1989
JongHyun (김종현) April 8, 1990
Key (김기범) September 23, 1991
MinHo (최민호) December 9, 1991
TaeMin (이태민) July 18, 1993

KOREAN ALBUMS
The Shinee World (2008)
Lucifer (2010)
Chapter 1. Dream Girl—The Misconceptions of
   You (2013)
Chapter 2. Why So Serious?—The Misconceptions
   of Me (2013)
The Misconceptions of Us (2013)

KOREAN MINI-ALBUMS
Replay (2008)
Romeo (2009)
2009: Year of Us (2009)
Sherlock (2012)
Everybody (2013)

JAPANESE ALBUMS
The First (2011)
Boys Meet U (2013)

FAN CLUB Shawol (SHINee World)
OFFICIAL COLOR Pearl aqua green

It was a look that went well with SM's typical upbeat, cute style of music. Around 2010, the group changed its image slightly, getting rougher and tougher. (Check out the Mohawk on Key in the "Lucifer" video.) More recently, it has changed yet again, opting for a mature and grown-up look, which is probably fitting given that the members are all older.

Like many SM Entertainment groups, SHINee has found huge fan bases around Asia, and done especially well in Japan. In 2011, SHINee became the first non-Japanese group ever to place three singles into the top three of the Oricon weekly singles chart. And the group's 2013 tour has taken them to many of Japan's largest stadiums.

ZE:A

Star Empire Entertainment

Ze:A, an abbreviation of "Jeguk-ui Aideul," or "Children of Empire" in Korean, has grown a big following around Asia since its 2010 debut. In Korea, the group built its initial following through dozens of guerrilla concerts and appearances all over the country, creating a grassroots fan base. But Ze:A has from the beginning also worked hard on building fans all around Asia, thanks in part to the group's diversity of language skills. Indeed, even before its debut, the group had signed with Warner Music China and Sony to further promotions around Asia.

With nine members, Ze:A boasts a diverse line-up of talent, with several members acting on TV and in films as well as hosting variety programs,

MEMBERS
Kevin (Kim Ji-yeop; 김지엽) February 23, 1988
Kwanghee (Hwang Kwang-hee; 황광희) August 25, 1988
Siwan (Yim Si-wan; 임시완) December 1, 1988
Junyoung (Moon Jun-young; 문준영) February 9, 1989 (leader)
Taeheon (Kim Tae-heon; 김태헌) June 18, 1989
Heechul (Jung Hee-cheol; 정희철) December 9, 1989
Minwoo (Ha Min-woo; 하민우) September 6, 1990
Hyungsik (Park Hyung-sik; 박형식) November 16, 1991
Dongjun (Kim Dong-jun; 김동준) February 11, 1992

SUBGROUPS
Ze:A Five
Ze:A 4U

KOREAN ALBUMS
Lovability (2011)
Spectaculary (2012)

JAPANESE ALBUMS
Ze:A! (2010)
Phoenix (2012)

JAPANESE MINI-ALBUM
Here I Am (2011)

TAIWANESE ALBUMS
Di Guo Jing Xuan (2010)
My Only Wish (2011, EP)

THAI ALBUM
Thailand Thank You (2011, EP)

FAN CLUB Ze:A's (Ze:A Style)
OFFICIAL COLOR Pearl gold

The guys in Ze:A have been nearly as successful as solo artists and entertainers as they have been as a group.

Hyungsik   Junyoung   Kevin   Kwanghee   Minwoo

starring in musicals, and much more. Minwoo is even a member of another group, 3Peace Lovers, a Japan-based band that includes Nikaido Hayato and Sasake Yoshihide.

With so much on the go, it's amazing that the guys are able to record and perform together as much as they do. Which is one reason Ze:A has generated two subgroups, Ze:A Five and Ze:A 4U,

so fans can continue to enjoy the group even when all nine members are not available. Despite its various forms, you can be sure Ze:A will continue to play great catchy, fun music for all its fans.

Heechul

Siwan

Dongjun

Taeheon

Kara, shown here at its first solo concert in 2012, has become one of the biggest girl groups in K-pop, thanks to its hit songs and great style.

Sooyoung

Tiffany

Hyoyeon

MEMBERS
Taeyeon (김태연) March 9, 1989
Jessica (정수연) April 18, 1989
Sunny (이순규) May 15, 1989
Tiffany (황미영) August 1, 1989
Hyoyeon (김효연) September 22, 1989
Yuri (권유리) December 5, 1989
Sooyoung (최수영) February 10, 1990
Yoona (임윤아) May 30, 1990
Seohyun (서주현) June 28, 1991

SUBGROUP
Girls' Generation-TaeTiSeo (Taeyeon, Tiffany, Seohyun)

KOREAN ALBUMS
Girls' Generation (2007)
Oh! (2010)
The Boys (2011)
I Got a Boy (2013)

KOREAN MINI-ALBUMS
Gee (2009)
Tell Me Your Wish (Genie) (2009)
Hoot (2010)

JAPANESE ALBUMS
Girls' Generation (2011)
Girls & Peace (2012)

FAN CLUB S♥NE (So-One)
OFFICIAL COLOR Pastel rose

GIRLS' GENERATION

SM Entertainment

Before summer 2012 turned the world of K-pop upside-down, Girls' Generation was the biggest K-pop group on YouTube, led by their light and bubbly "Gee," which now has more than 100 million views. The nine-member girl group featured some of the catchiest songs and dances in K-pop, not to mention some of the leggiest videos.

Formed in 2007, Girls' Generation, called Sonyeo Sidae (소녀시대) in Korean, was in many

ways SM Entertainment's female answer to Super Junior, a large, upbeat K-pop group that could appeal to the widest possible audience. Jessica, Sooyoung and Hyoyeon joined SM in 2000, and the other members slowly came together over the years, with Sunny being the last to join, in 2007, although she had been a trainee with SM way back in 1998.

The group started out quite well, but nothing could compare to the leap it took in 2009 with "Gee." Exploding with *aegyo* (Korean for "cuteness"), "Gee" quickly rocketed up the charts, smashing records left and right. It followed that song with more hits, like "Tell Me Your Wish (Genie)" and "Run Devil Run," but the Teddy Riley-produced "The Boys" in 2011 would become its biggest hit since "Gee."

Not surprisingly, Girls' Generation has also done exceptionally well outside of Korea. The group began promotions in Japan in 2010, and its debut album there, *Girls' Generation*, was the fifth biggest seller of 2011 and the highest by a Korean group. It also got a nod from America's *Spin* magazine.

Since then, the legend of Girls' Generation has kept growing. The group appeared on *Late Night With David Letterman* in early 2012, then on French television, and an English-language album has long been rumored. Along with

Whether in dresses, sportswear or short shorts, Girls' Generation always presents a fresh, fun image.

that push into America, Girls' Generation earned a lot of the early attention from the Western press, both before Psy came along and after, and the group was a major focus of *The New Yorker*'s big profile of K-pop in October 2012.

Five members of the group now have songwriting credits to their names, a sign that their abilities are continuing to grow.

Like many K-pop groups these days, Girls' Generation also has its sub-unit, Girls Generation-TTS (or TaeTiSeo, as in Taeyeon, Tiffany and Seohyun). It has done well so far, with its first single, "Twinkle," charting in Korea and Japan and on *Billboard*'s world chart.

Girl groups have always been an important part of the foundation of K-pop, with huge stars like FinKL, S.E.S., Baby Vox and others. But by the mid-2000s, most of those

groups had disbanded or seen their popularity fade. Girls' Generation, together with the Wonder Girls, brought back the all-girl group, re-establishing the importance of girl groups in the K-pop scene.

Given that Girls' Generation beat out many of the top pops acts in the world to win the Video of the Year at the first YouTube Music Awards in late 2013, the group's future looks limitless.

Girls' Generation takes the cake.

2NE1

YG Entertainment

Feisty, unconventional and full of swagger, 2NE1 is perhaps the most rocking girl group in K-pop. Founded by YG Entertainment to be a "female Big Bang," the 2NE1 girls trained for four years before their 2009 debut with Big Bang in "Lollipop," a song that doubled as an advertisement for LG's Cyon phone. In "Lollipop," both groups wore all bright colors, reminiscent of H.O.T's debut "Candy," way back in the 1990s, but soon after that 2NE1 grew more edgy and unconventional.

Starting from its first single, "Fire," in 2009, 2NE1 has consistently pushed a harder, bolder sound than any other girl group in Korea. "I Don't Care" showed that the group also had a softer side, but the dominant theme throughout 2NE1's career has always been swag.

The young women who make up 2NE1 come from diverse backgrounds. CL grew up in France and

2NE1 performing at the DMZ Documentary Film Festival in 2011.

Flashy and brash, 2NE1 has some of the loudest and most fun styles in K-pop.

MEMBERS
CL (Lee Chaerin; 이채린) February 26, 1991 (leader)
Bom (Park Bom; 박봄) March 24, 1984
Dara (Park Sandara; 박산다라) November 12, 1984
Minzy (Gong Minji; 공민지) January 18, 1994

KOREAN ALBUMS
To Anyone (2010)
Tba (2013)

KOREAN MINI-ALBUMS
2NE1 (2009)
2NE1 2nd Mini Album (2011)

JAPANESE ALBUMS
Collection (2012)

SOLO ALBUM
CL: "Baddest Female" (2013)

FAN CLUBS Blackjack (Korea), Blackjack Nolza (Japan)
OFFICIAL COLOR Hot pink

Minzy

Dara

Bom

CL

Japan because of her physicist father's job. Dara spent many years in the Philippines, where she entered talent programs and released music of her own. Bom lived in the United States for a time and even entered the Berklee College of Music before getting the nod from YG. Minzy, who is a full ten years younger than Bom and Sandara, grew up in Gwangju, Jeolla province, where her emphasis on dance helped her capture the attention of YG.

It was 2NE1's 2011 single "I Am the Best" from its second EP that really defined the group. Boastful and brash, "I Am the Best" featured perhaps the wildest video in all of K-pop, with plenty of leather and spikes, crazy hair and heavy weaponry. It racked up more than 80 million views on YouTube.

Let's say it was the wildest until CL released her own solo album in 2013, led by the uber swag "The Baddest Female." A K-pop star wearing a gold grill with vampire teeth? Crazy. In fact, it may have been too crazy of K-pop, with its bare-bones beats and austere sound and there was quite a reaction against "Baddest Female."

CL is the leader of 2NE1 and is rapidly becoming an icon in her own right. (In the world of K-pop, gays and lesbians love CL as much as they love Robyn in Western pop music.) CL has also helped change how YG develops female stars. In her early days, the company pushed CL to have plastic surgery, but she refused. Today, YG says it has stopped pushing its stars to have plastic surgery.

2NE1 returned to the scene soon after CL's solo album and released a slew of new singles in the second half of 2013. This time, the much more poppy and listener-friendly tracks, "Falling in Love" and "Do You Love Me," hit the sweet spot, reminding the group's fans why they love 2NE1 so much.

WONDER GIRLS

JYP Entertainment

You could be forgiven for thinking that the Wonder Girls weren't going to make it. Their first single, "Irony," in early 2007 didn't do much and disappeared quickly from the scene. Founding member Hyuna withdrew from the group in July, citing health problems.

But, wow, did that all change with the Wonder Girls' second single, "Tell Me." First, Yubin replaced Hyuna in the group. Then, in October, JYP Entertainment released the Wonder Girls' first full-length album and right away they knew they had a major hit on

MEMBERS
Sunye (Min Sun-ye; 민선예) August 12, 1989 (leader)
Yubin (Park Yu-bin; 박유빈) October 4, 1988
Yenny (Park Ye-eun; 박예은) May 26, 1989
Lim (Woo Hye-lim; 우혜림) September 1, 1992
Sohee (Ahn So-hee; 안소희) June 27, 1992

PAST MEMBERS
Hyuna (Kim Hyun-a; 김현아)
Sunmi (Lee Sun-mi; 이선미)

KOREAN ALBUMS
The Wonder Years (2007)
Wonder World (2011)

KOREAN MINI-ALBUMS
The Wonder Years: Trilogy (2008)
Wonder Party (2012)

JAPANESE ALBUMS
Nobody for Everybody (2012)

FAN CLUB Wonderful
OFFICIAL COLOR Pearl burgundy

Wonder Girls first attracted acclaim with their catchy single "Tell Me."

The Wonder Girls—Sunye, Yenny, Yubin, Sunmi and Sohee—sporting a 1960s retro Motown look in 2008.

their hands. "Tell Me" was huge, thanks to a catchy Stacy Q sample from the 1980s song "Two of Hearts" and a signature dance that was fun to copy. The song zoomed up to No. 1 on Korea's charts and stayed there for weeks.

It wasn't long before the Wonder Girls had another major hit, the 1960s-influenced "Nobody." Released in 2008, "Nobody" saw the Wonder Girls now sporting a retro look, like something out of Motown but incredibly rich and stylish. It was stylish enough that the influential blogger Perez Hilton picked up on it, calling the video "so fab" and giving the song a major push in the West. Soon, the Wonder Girls was opening for the Jonas Brothers on their America tour, performing the English version of its hit "Nobody." By fall 2009, the English language version had actually made it onto *Billboard*'s Hot 100 singles chart—the main chart, that is, not the K-pop chart or anything else. Eventually, the song made it up to No. 76, nothing to frighten Beyonce, but for K-pop it was an amazing, tantalizing taste of what success in the West could mean.

Since then, JYP Entertainment has put a lot of its energies into pushing Wonder Girls in the West.

In 2010, Wonder Girls entered the Chinese market with its compilation album *Wonder Girls*, which included Chinese language versions of "Tell Me," "Nobody" and "So Hot."

Although the group got its own made-for-TV movie on Teen Nick in 2012, it was never able to make the leap up to the next level, and some of its fans in Korea and Asia complained of feeling forgotten.

It's also worth noting that the Wonder Girls have gotten involved in some of the songwriting for their group. Yenny has been the biggest contributor, with her name on the credits for eight songs. And Yubin even helped update the classic "The Beauty" (*Miin*), a Shin Joong-hyun rock song from the 1970s.

Now that Sunye has gotten married and had a baby, the rest of the Wonder Girls are concentrating on their solo careers. It's so rare that real life intrudes upon the magical world of K-pop that sometimes even something as normal as marriage and motherhood can seem surprising. But with so many passionate fans, there is no telling what the future might hold for the Wonder Girls, "the girls who can amaze the world."

One of the most iconic images of the Wonder Girls from the peak of the group's "Nobody" phase.

After working hard to break into the US market, the Wonder Girls starred in a made-for-TV movie for Teen Nick in February 2012.

The Wonder Girls endorsed a street basketball video game in 2008.

4MINUTE

Cube Entertainment

Two years after leaving Wonder Girls, Hyuna was back in the K-pop spotlight, now part of the girl group 4Minute, along with fellow JYP Entertainment alumna Ji-hyun, 4Minute's leader. The other three members were introduced in the weeks that followed and then 4Minute's first mini-album came out in June 2009.

From the beginning, Cube Entertainment was very active in pushing 4Minute internationally, recording with American artist Amerie for the Asian release of her fourth album, touring Hong Kong, Thailand, Taiwan and more in 2010, and releasing its first Japanese single in May 2010.

Cube has made a point of co-ordinating its artists' releases, so 4Minute, Beast and G.Na often tour together and sing on each other's tracks. They've held concerts together around the world, in London, China, Brazil (in the first paid-ticket K-pop concert

In a K-pop world full of cuteness, 4Minute, comprising So-hyun, Ga-yoon, Hyun-a, Ji-hyun and Ji-yoon, often shows a more mature side than other groups.

4Minute performing live at the Dream Concert in 2011.

MEMBERS
Nam Ji-hyun (남지현) January 9, 1990 (leader)
Heo Ga-yoon (허가윤) May 18, 1990
Jeon Ji-yoon (전지윤) October 15, 1990
Kim Hyun-a (김현아) June 6, 1992
Kwon So-hyun (권소현) August 30, 1994

SUBGROUP
2Yoon (Ga-yoon, Ji-yoon)

KOREAN ALBUMS
4Minutes Left (2011)

KOREAN MINI-ALBUMS
For Muzik (2009)
Hit Your Heart (2010)
Heart to Heart (2011)
Volume Up (2012)
Name Is 4Minute (2013)

JAPANESE ALBUMS
Diamond (2010)

SOLO MINI-ALBUMS
Hyuna:
Bubble Pop! (2011)
Trouble Maker (2011)
Melting (2012)

FAN CLUB 4NIA
OFFICIAL COLOR Pearl purple

in South America) and, more recently, in Malaysia.

So far, 2013 has been 4Minute's best year yet, as its album *Name Is 4Minute* spurred the group's most successful single to date, "What's Your Name?" A surprise single released in late June, "Is It Poppin'?," turned into one of the biggest songs of the summer.

Even while a member of 4Minute, Hyuna has had a very successful solo career, gaining fame—and some infamy—for her sexy vixen image. The ridiculous and infectious "Bubble Pop" received plenty of attention in the West, and has racked up 56 million views on YouTube. But her biggest claim to fame is being the women Psy dances with in "Gangnam Style," earning her a gazillion views on YouTube. Her version of the song "Oppa Is Just My Style" has also gained a respectable 385 million views.

Ga-yoon and Ji-yoon have teamed up to form a 4Minute subgroup called 2Yoon. Their EP *Harvest Moon*, released in early 2013, did fairly well, earning some note for a rare K-pop foray into the world of country music, well, K-pop-style quasi country.

AFTER SCHOOL

Pledis Entertainment

After School is a rare
K-pop group that openly
changes its members.

While the composition of most K-pop groups is fiercely guarded, After School has gone in the opposite direction, freely letting new girls come and go as needed. Since After School's debut at the end of 2008 as a five-member group, three members have left and six have joined. With three sub-units within the group, After School is one of the busiest K-pop acts around.

Initially modeled on the Pussycat Dolls—showing plenty of skin and sultriness—After School caught on quickly, winning many new artist awards in 2009 in Korea and Japan.

Since then, the group has also gone on to build big fan followings all over Asia, as well as Europe and South America.

From its inception, After School was never shy about going for the big concept. The girls have tap danced, cane danced, performed a drum line and even tackled the physically challenging art of pole dancing on the 2013 release, "First Love" (injuring three members in the process, luckily not seriously), confirming them as K-pop's top performers.

Orange Caramel has been a successful subgroup, nearly as

popular as After School itself, presenting a slightly younger and cuter image. After School Red and Blue further divide the group, with Red (Jungah, Uee, Nana and Kahi) going for a sexier style, and Blue (Jooyeon, Raina, Lizzy and E-Young) more fresh and cute.

Rahi, who graduated from the group in 2012, has had a long career as a successful dancer in Korea, having worked with many leading artists like DJ D.O.C. and BoA, before becoming the leader of After School. Although she has now left the group, her solo career continues to go strongly.

After School at a music festival on New Year's Eve 2011.

MEMBERS

Jungah (Kim Jung-ah; 김정아) August 2, 1983 (leader)
Jooyeon (Lee Joo-yeon; 이주연) March 19, 1987
Uee (Kim Yu-jin; 김유진) April 9, 1988
Raina (Oh Hye-rin; 오혜린) May 7, 1989
Nana (Im Jin-ah; 임 진아) September 14, 1991
Lizzy (Park Soo-young; 박수영) July 31, 1992
E-Young (Noh Yi-young; 노이영) August 16, 1992
Kaeun (Lee Ka-eun; 이가은) August 20, 1994

GRADUATED MEMBERS

Soyoung (Yoo So-young; 유소영)
Bekah (Rebekah Kim; 레베카 김)
Rahi (Park Ji-young; 박지영)

SUBGROUPS

Orange Caramel (Raina, Nana, Lizzy)
After School Blue (Jooyeon, Raina, Lizzy, E-young)
After School Red (Jungah, Uee, Nana, Kahi)

KOREAN ALBUM

Virgin (2011)

JAPANESE ALBUM

Playgirlz (2012)
Orange Caramel
Lipstick (2012)
Orange Caramel (Japan)

FAN CLUB Play Girlz
OFFICIAL COLOR Yellow

BROWN EYED GIRLS

Nega Network

Brown Eyed Girls stands out in K-pop, especially among female groups, for how the members have taken control of their music and careers. The group wasn't formed by a management team but instead was put together by group leader JeA. They write many of their own songs. In fact, Miryo is the most prolific female songwriter in all of K-pop. And they aren't shy about presenting adult, grown-up messages about life and love, sometimes far from the bubbly,

cutesy world that dominates much of K-pop.

JeA had played in a rock band in high school and written and sung songs for television soundtracks for several years under her real name, Kim Hyo-jin. But her attempts at becoming a K-pop star hadn't panned out until one day she was asked by Nega Network to form a new group. So JeA got in touch with Miryo, a young rapper, and asked her to join, followed by Narsha, who had been a friend of

hers from high school, and lastly the youngest member, Ga-in.

The four women trained together for three years, originally under the name Crescendo, before releasing their first album. But its generic R&B sound did not make much of an impact, especially as the group deliberately kept their images off the early promotions, opting for a blank-slate marketing campaign. Their next release, an EP called *With L.O.V.E*, did better, as did their second full album.

Brown Eyed Girls is one of the most grown-up girl groups in K-pop, and its members (clockwise from top) Ga-in, Miryo, Narsha and JeA, are quite active in shaping their music.

The members of Brown Eyed Girls are quite diverse, with interesting solo projects.

But Brown Eyed Girls really took off with *Sound-G* in 2009, which changed its style to more of an electronic dance sound and the look of the girls to one that was more provocative and sexy. That album also featured the group's fantastically popular single "Abracadabra," which became one of the biggest hits of the year. You might recognize the main dance move in the video for "Abracadabra," a hypnotic hip shake that was adopted by Psy for his "Gentleman" video.

Since then, Brown Eyed Girls has been a top K-pop group, but the individual members have also had great success. Narsha released a solo album in 2010. Miryo's solo album came out in 2012 and, as mentioned, she has been incredibly productive writing for other groups. JeA is actually the second most prolific female K-pop songwriter and she has also recorded with numerous other artists and released her solo album in 2013.

But Ga-in has been the most successful solo artist, having released three solo mini-albums and numerous singles, including the big hit *Talk About S* in 2012. *Talk About S*, especially its single "Bloom," was surprisingly adult and frank about sex, earning an adults-only rating in Korea, but it was more than just a sleazy, leering exploitive song and video. "Bloom" was positive, mature and empowering, a rare combination in any country's pop music.

In July 2013, the four members of Brown Eyed Girls finally had their long-awaited group return with *Black Box*, an album that records their journey.

DAVICHI

Core Contents Media

Davichi has been a popular duo in K-pop since 2008 when it dominated the rookie awards.

Davichi is one of the very rare duos in K-pop, having built a large fan following with its simple, acoustic-based songs and strong singing. The style of Davichi focuses on melodies and singing rather than the typical flash and bang of most K-pop, but, make no mistake about it, the twosome is still big-time and has played to sizeable crowds from Vietnam to Chile.

Davichi made its debut in 2008 with the ballad "I Love You Even Though I Hate You," which featured a dramatic and elaborate video that starred singing superstar Lee Hyori and actress Lee Mi-yeon as two women who had just been released from prison.

Since then, Davichi has gone from hit to hit. Its second studio album, *Mystic Ballad*, released in March 2013, was its biggest success yet, and was almost immediately followed by a new hit single in July, "Missing You Today."

MEMBERS
Lee Haeri (이해리) February 14, 1985
Kang Min-kyung (강민경) August 3, 1990

KOREAN ALBUMS
Amaranth (2008)
Mystic Ballad (2013)

KOREAN MINI-ALBUMS
Davichi in Wonderland (2009)
Innocence (2010)
Love Delight (2011)

FAN CLUB Girls High
OFFICIAL COLOR n/a

"Missing You Today" by Davichi duo Min-kyung and Haeri held off the mighty 2NE1 in the summer of 2013 on the *Billboard* K-pop chart.

SM Entertainment

Probably the most electronic and
edgy group SM Entertainment has
ever produced is f(x), pushing the
conservative boundaries of Korea's
leading music label. In 2013, it even
became the first K-pop group to
play at the SXSW music festival in
Texas, a raucous and sprawling
music fest that features thousands
of bands, usually of the rock variety.

Let's not overstate things, of
course—f(x) is definitely K-pop. But
it could be growing into the next
great K-pop super group.

Like most of SM Entertainment's
groups, f(x) started out with a bang
in the fall of 2009, and it wasn't
long before the group was
performing in Japan, Paris and
elsewhere. Songs like "Pinocchio"
and "Hot Summer" did well, and
the girls' popularity kept growing.

The group's big leap came in
2012 with its second mini-album,
Electric Shock, led by the single of
the same name. The propulsive,
crackling "Electric Shock" jolted
fans, earning more than 52 million
YouTube views, vaulting the band
ever higher in the K-pop hierarchy.

As popular as "Electric Shock"
was, *Pink Tape* was probably even
more so, reaching No. 1 on
Billboard's World Album chart.
"Rum Pum Pum Pum" may have

One of the most unusual and edgy looks of all the
SM Entertainment acts is f(x).

Victoria

Luna

been the lead single, but other tracks on the album, such as "Airplane," were a lot stronger. SM Entertainment is famous for having a particular house style, but f(x) on *Pink Tape* showed a willingness to push SM's boundaries with a bigger, edgier sound.

Krystal is the younger sister of Girls' Generation's Jessica, and has been working with SM from when she was just five years old (she had a small appearance in a Shinhwa music video). Of course, she was too young to be a trainee then, but over the years she appeared in several television commercials before her parents finally allowed her to join SM Entertainment full-time in 2006.

MEMBERS
Victoria February 2, 1987 (leader)
Amber September 18, 1992
Luna (박선영) August 12, 1993
Sulli (최진리) March 29, 1994
Krystal (정수정) October 24, 1994

KOREAN ALBUMS
Pinocchio (2011)
Pink Tape (2013)

KOREAN MINI-ALBUMS
Nu ABO (2010)
Electric Shock (2012)

And with Chinese member Victoria and Taiwanese-American Amber, f(x) is yet another symbol of how seriously SM takes the Chinese and international markets for their music. In fact, when f(x) made its debut, SM described it as an "Asian dance pop group," not a Korean one. Does that still make them K-pop? Or is SM-pop a new genre?

Krystal

Sulli

Amber

KARA

DSP Media

Kara's debut, *The First Blooming*, in 2007 didn't exactly set the K-pop world on fire. Maybe it was the pressure to become the next FinKL, the classic K-pop group also started by DSP Media, or maybe it was just the wrong sound for the time, but its first album was a bit of a dud. Soon after, parental pressure forced Kim Sung-hee out of the group and new members, Goo Ha-ra and Kang Ji-young, joined, injecting the group with a burst of energy.

MEMBERS
Park Gyu-ri (박규리) May 21, 1988
Han Seung-yeon (한승연) July 24, 1988
Goo Ha-ra (구하라) January 13, 1991
Nicole Yong-joo Jung (정영주) October 7, 1991
Kang Ji-young (강지영) January 18, 1994

PAST MEMBER
Kim Sung-hee

KOREAN ALBUMS
The First Blooming (2007)
Revolution (2009)
Step (2011)

KOREAN MINI-ALBUMS
Rock U (2008)
Pretty Girl (2008)
Honey (2009)
Lupin (2010)
Jumping (2010)
Pandora (2012)

JAPANESE ALBUMS
Girl's Talk (2010)
Super Girl (2011)
Girls Forever (2012)

FAN CLUB Kamilia
OFFICIAL COLOR Pearl peach

For the past three years, Kara has been one of the most successful K-pop acts in Japan.

Ji-young, Nicole, Gyu-ri, Seung-yeon and Ha-ra performing at a concert in Seoul in February 2012.

The extended play *Rock U* did a bit better, and *Pretty Girl* better still. With *Honey* in 2009, Kara finally got its first No. 1 hit.

By the time Kara's second full album, *Revolution*, was released in mid-2009, the group had finally found its identity, expressed by a fun, party vibe. Its third single from *Revolution*, "Mister," was the group's biggest hit, thanks in part to a popular "butt dance" that went with it.

When the song was released in Japan, it did particularly well (Oricon said it was the best debut by a girl group in nearly 30 years), and suddenly Kara was well on its way to becoming a leader in K-pop's rise in Japan. Over the last three years, Kara has won plenty of awards in Japan and held one sold-out concert after another.

However, Kara nearly missed out on its fabulous success, coming to the verge of breaking up in early 2011 when four members of the group (all except for Gyu-ri) announced that they wanted out of their contracts with DSP. Fans were shocked and worried that this would turn into another TVXQ! and possibly end another promising K-pop group. Things were looking really bad at first, but after three months of furious negotiations, DSP and all the members of Kara came to an understanding, the lawsuit was withdrawn and Kara was soon recording and performing again.

Since then, Kara has been better than ever and, fortunately for the Kamilias, they look like they will be singing for some time to come.

MISS A

JYP Entertainment

Miss A ready for a business meeting.

Miss A was JYP Entertainment's attempt at creating a girl group with the China market in mind. What had started as a five-member "Chinese Wonder Girls," as JYP Entertainment sometimes called them, changed as the concept developed, with two original members leaving and Hyerim (who is Korean but grew up in Hong Kong) moving to the actual Wonder Girls. Koreans Suzy and then Min joined in 2009, and by 2010 the group, now called Miss A, was ready for its debut single.

Like a lot of groups these days, including Big Bang and 2NE1, Miss A actually started with an advertising campaign for Samsung Anycall. Just a week later, the group released its first real single, "Bad Girl, Good Girl," which quickly topped the charts, followed by its second song, "Breathe," which also did well. Then, in 2011, Miss A released its first full-length album, *A Class*, which included its most popular song yet, "Goodbye Baby."

Since then, Miss A has kept up a regular supply of juicy singles, even as the individual members have grown busier and busier with their own projects, whether on TV or in advertising (or, for Fei and Jia, back in China).

Despite the group not appointing an official "leader," Suzy appears to be turning into Miss A's break-out star, thanks to a series of high-profile acting roles. She was the lead of the popular TV series *Dream High* in 2011, the well-regarded movie *Architecture 101*, and the even more successful television drama *Gu Family Book* in 2013. Today, she is on the verge of having two million Twitter followers, by far the greatest number among K-pop female artists.

MEMBERS
Fei (Wang Fei Fei) April 27, 1987
Jia (Meng Jia) February 3, 1989
Min (Lee Min-young; 이민영) June 23, 1991
Suzy (Bae Su-ji; 배수지) October 10, 1994

KOREAN ALBUMS
A Class (2011)
Hush (2013)

KOREAN MINI-ALBUMS
Touch (2012)
Independent Women Part III (2012)

FAN CLUB Say A
OFFICIAL COLOR n/a

Jia, Min, Fei and Suzy of Miss A, JYP Entertainment's strongest push yet into the China market.

Miss A can also rock the crazy cute outfits.

SECRET

TS Entertainment

In many ways, Secret is one of the most representative K-pop girl groups, with four attractive young women using catchy, sweet songs and plenty of cuteness to drive audiences into a frenzy.

The group is led by Hyo-sung, who had been obsessed with dancing and music from young but failed her first auditions. Only in 2005 did she pass an audition and then joined a reality TV program, *Battle Shinhwa*. Her success on that show led to her first contract, but that company was never able to get the group off the ground, and by 2008 she was out of the business again. Finally, TS Entertainment contacted her and soon Secret was on its way, with three other members.

From "I Want You Back" to "Magic" to "Madonna," none of Secret's songs were ground-breaking, but they kept making steady progress. The group also moved quickly to promote itself in Japan and soon built a sizeable following there as well.

Finally, in 2012, with the single "Poison," Secret climbed to the next level. The single that followed, "Talk That," began to earn the

MEMBERS
Jeon Hyo-sung (전효성) October 13, 1989 (leader)
Jung Ha-na (정하나) February 2, 1990 (formerly Zinger)
Song Ji-eun (송지은) May 5, 1990
Han Sun-hwa (한선화) October 6, 1990

KOREAN ALBUMS
Moving in Secret (2011)

KOREAN MINI-ALBUMS
Secret Time (2010)
Madonna (2010)
Poison (2012)
Letter From Secret (2013)

JAPANESE ALBUM
Welcome to Secret Time (2012)

JAPANESE MINI-ALBUM
Shy Boy (2011)

FAN CLUB Secret Time
OFFICIAL COLOR n/a

group better critical praise as their style got more sophisticated, going beyond just cute or sexy.

Secret may not be revolutionizing K-pop, but the group is a fine example of the high standard of pop that Korea is putting out today.

The secret's out. Secret is a great K-pop act.

They're cute,
they're catchy,
they're Secret.

Secret performing at a K-pop fashion
show-cum-event in 2012.

SISTAR

Starship Entertainment

MEMBERS
Hyolyn (Kim Hyo-jung; 김효정) January 11, 1991
Bora (Yoon Bo-ra; 윤보라) January 30, 1990
Soyou (Kang Ji-hyun; 강지현) February 12, 1992
Dasom (Kim Da-som; 김다솜) May 6, 1993

SUBGROUP
Sistar 19 (Hyorin, Bora)

KOREAN ALBUMS
So Cool (2011)
Give It to Me (2013)

KOREAN MINI-ALBUMS
Alone (2012)
Loving U (2012)

SISTAR 19 SINGLES
Ma Boy (2011)
Girl Not Around Any Longer (2013)

FAN CLUB Star 1
OFFICIAL COLOR Fuschia

Sistar is definitely a group on the rise, having consistently grown in popularity since its 2010 debut. Each of its first three singles that year did better than the last on the charts, with "How Dare You?" giving the group its first No. 1.

The pulsing electro of "So Cool," the title track from its first album in 2011, was one of Sistar's biggest hits, pulling in 31 million views on YouTube, helped, no doubt, by plenty of short skirts and deep-bending dance moves, and was ranked one of the top K-pop songs of the year.

The next year, "Alone," another Brave Brothers production, also did very well, reaching No. 1 on all the charts and setting the record for the longest stint at No. 1 on the *Billboard* K-pop album chart. "Loving U" was also a big hit.

Despite being so new, Sistar has, naturally, already got a subgroup: Sister19. Comprised of just Hyolyn and Bora, Sistar19 has released just two singles, but both have performed well.

With its second album, *Give It to Me*, released in June 2013, Sistar once again pulled in a haul of No. 1's on the charts, despite facing some of the stiffest competition ever in K-pop. Sistar may not be in the top echelon of K-pop groups yet, but if the group keeps racking up hits, it won't be long before it is.

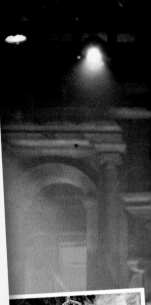

Sistar, comprised of Dasom, Bora, Hyolyn and Soyou, may have started out slowly, but the group's popularity keeps growing.

T-ARA

Core Contents Media

T-ara started out as a five-member group before losing two members, then gaining three, then gaining one more who left the group just a year later, making it a six-member group today.

Although T-ara did not start well in 2009, the group quickly improved

and by the end of the year it was picking up plenty of rookie awards and rising up the charts. "Roly Poly" was one of the biggest singles of 2011, and in Japan "Bo Peep Bo Beep" became the first debut single by a non-Japanese girl group to hit No. 1. Arguably, the group's 2012 single "Lovey Dovey" was even bigger.

T-ara was also the center of one of the more compelling and notable "scandals" in K-pop in recent years, the apparent bullying of member Hwayoung. In July

2012, Hwayoung's contract was suddenly terminated with the management company, leading to speculation about what might have happened. Rumors quickly circulated that Hwayoung had been bullied out of the group—and the music label. Or perhaps she had acted unprofessionally and needed to be fired. With the issue now well into the past and no one talking about it anymore, the truth will probably never be known. But the Hwayoung issue was an important reminder that K-pop idols are human, as are members of their

MEMBERS
Boram (Jeon Bo-ram; 전보람) March 22, 1986
Qri (Lee Ji-hyun; 이지현) December 12, 1986
So Yeon (Park So-yeon; 박소연) October 5, 1987
Eun Jung (Ham Eun-jung; 함은정) December 12, 1988
Hyomin (Park Sun-young; 박선영) May 30, 1989
Jiyeon (Park Ji-yeon; 박지연) June 7, 1993
Dani (Kim Dan) (in training)

PAST MEMBERS
Areum (Lee A-reum; 이아름)
Hwayoung (Ryu Hwa-young; 류화영)
Jiwon (Yang Ji-won; 양지원)
Jiae (Kim Ji-ae; 김지애)

SUBGROUPS
T-ara N4 (Jiyeon, Hyomin, Dani, Eun Jung)
QBS (Qri, Boram, So Yeon); focused on Japan

KOREAN ALBUM
First Album (2009)

KOREAN MINI-ALBUMS
Temptastic (2010)
John Travolta Wannabe (2011)
Black Eyes (2011)
Day by Day (2012)

JAPANESE ALBUMS
Jewelry Box (2012)
Treasure Box (2013)

FAN CLUBS Queens (Korea), Sweet Treasure
(Japan)
OFFICIAL COLOR Pearl ivory

T-ara's "Sexy Love" featuring Eun Jung, Hyomin, Qri, Boram, So Yeon, Jiyeon and Dani, was one of the more memorable girl groups as living mannequins music videos.

management companies, and are subject to the same pressures and fears as you or I.

Today, T-ara continues to shine. Subgroup T-ara N4 scored a bit hit in the spring of 2013 with the catchy "Jeonwon Diary." QBS is another subgroup consisting of members not in N4, and is focused on the Japanese market.

T-ara N4 has its eyes on Western markets, with an English-language single on the way.

CHAPTER 5

SOLO ARTISTS

He's got Gangnam Style, he's a Gentlemen, he's a champion—he's Psy.

PSY

YG Entertainment

It is strange, isn't it, that Korea's biggest K-pop sensation can barely be classified as K-pop? Park Jae-sang's goofy, fun-loving techno/rap music has long been a style unto itself in Korea. But against all odds, somehow in 2012 the rest of the world got the joke. Boy did they ever—1.8 billion YouTube views and still going strong!

An inveterate joker and music fan, Jae-sang was never much one for studying. So when his business-man father sent him to Boston University to study business, it wasn't long before Jae-sang dropped out, bought a lot of music equipment and entered the Berklee College of Music. But even Berklee involved too much studying for the young Jae-sang, so he left that school and returned to Korea, where he was soon working on his own music career.

It wasn't long before Jae-sang attracted the attention of Korea's music industry. He rebranded himself as "Psy," and in 2001 released his first album. In a sign of what was to come, *Psy From the Psycho World* was catchy dance-rap, with plenty of fun hooks and samples. Take "Bird," for example, which was based heavily around a sample from Bananarama's version of "Venus" but with Psy rapping on top. The album greatly annoyed the authorities, who fined him for using naughty words and bad language. It wasn't even much of a hit and Psy himself didn't cut a very glamorous figure, but he wrote nearly all the songs himself and created a sound that didn't exist anywhere in Korea at the time.

FULL NAME
Park Jae-sang (박재상) December 31, 1977

KOREAN ALBUMS
Psy From the Psycho World (2001)
Ssa 2 (2002)
3 Mi (2002)
Ssajib (2006)
PsyFive (2010)

KOREAN MINI-ALBUMS
Psy 6 (Six Rules), Part 1 (2012)
Psy 6 (Six Rules), Part 2 (2013)

FAN CLUB Cho
OFFICIAL COLOR Black

Psy presenting "Gentleman" live in Seoul in April 2013.

A singer with a great sense of humor, Psy became one of the most unexpected icons ever.

His second album, *Ssa 2*, was more of the same, kicking off with "Shingoshik," a sexy dance track that featured heavy samples from Park Ji-yoon's classic track "Coming of Age Ceremony." The powers that be hated this album even more than his first, and had it banned for sale to people under nineteen.

Finally, with his third album, *3 Mi*, Psy had a genuine hit, "Champion," out just in time for the 2002 Korea–Japan World Cup (a huge event in Korea then, especially as Korea surprised the world and made it all the way to the semi-finals). Based on the famous Axel Foley theme from *Beverly Hills Cop*, "Champion," was the perfect Psy formula—catchy, odd and a lot of fun.

Sadly, just as Psy's career was hotting up, he ran into a series of major setbacks, most significantly military service. This is mandatory in Korea and in 2003 it was for twenty-six months. But Psy was able to get out of active service and instead worked for a software company, a pretty sweet assignment. He was discharged in 2005 and released his fourth album the next year. But not long after he was accused of not having fulfilled his duties to the country and was instead working on his music and personal projects. He had to enlist in the military *again* and this time he served in the regular Army.

Psy did his duty and, finally, in 2009, he was free again. Now, a lot of K-pop stars worry that their careers might wither while they are in the Army as fickle young people move on to the next thing. Imagine how Psy felt being mostly out of action for the better part of six years.

Upon returning to the music scene, Psy signed with YG Entertainment and released his fifth album. It did all right, but nothing spectacular.

Psy performing in Seoul
in October 2012 to
celebrate the incredible
international success of
"Gangnam Style."

Which brings us to the summer of 2012 when Psy released his sixth album, led by a single that you might have heard of, "Gangnam Style." Wow!

"Gangnam Style" came out in mid-July and in Korea it did okay, spending a couple of weeks on the top of the charts, but nothing unusual. But the thing is, this time Western social media caught on. Reddit took note of it on July 28, Gawker on July 30. Several celebrities tweeted about it. And the next thing you knew, a phenomenon was born.

People were surprised in August when Psy shot past Girls' Generation's "Gee" to become the most watched Korean video ever on YouTube. And "Gangnam Style" kept growing. One hundred million views. Two hundred million. By the end of 2012, it had zoomed past Justin Beiber's "Baby" to become the most watched YouTube video of all time, topping one billion views (although, strangely, it was only the third bestselling download of the year in the United States).

Psy's follow-up, "Gentleman," has done quite well so far,

although it is not the phenomenon that "Gangnam Style" was. But 575 million YouTube views is nothing to sniff at.

Since "Gangnam Style," life has been non-stop go-go-go for Psy, with endless TV appearances, meetings, concerts and more.

For all of Psy's success, his role in K-pop is as unclear as ever. In many ways, his success has pulled him even further from the core of K-pop. But as a YG Entertainment artist, he is also in the middle of K-pop. Which in many ways is a great metaphor of K-pop itself.

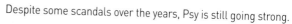

Despite some scandals over the years, Psy is still going strong.

BOA

SM Entertainment

If one singer has defined K-pop for the past decade, it would probably be BoA. Chosen by SM Entertainment when she was just eleven years old, BoA released her first album at thirteen and became a major star in Japan by fourteen. Since then, she has released a steady stream of hits in both countries. Today, BoA is just twenty-seven years old but has been a major K-pop star for more than half of her life.

Like many stars, it seems, BoA did not intend to become an idol. She actually was accompanying her brother to an SM Entertainment audition when she was scouted. The founder of SM Entertainment, Soo-Man Lee, saw her and liked her smile, and that was enough to give her a chance at stardom. Her first album, *ID: Peace B*, came out just two years later, but did not make much of an impact at the time.

But from the beginning, SM Entertainment also had its sights set on Japan. BoA was sent to Japan to live (with a news anchor) and be immersed in the language. In Japan, together with music

---

FULL NAME
Bo-a (권보아) November 5, 1986

KOREAN ALBUMS
ID: Peace B (2000)
No. 1 (2002)
Atlantis Princess (2003)
My Name (2004)
Girls on Top (2005)
Hurricane Venus (2010)
Only One (2012)

KOREAN MINI-ALBUMS
Jumping Into the World (2001)
Miracle (2002)
Shine We Are! (2003)

JAPANESE ALBUMS
Listen to My Heart (2002)
Valenti (2003)
Love & Honesty (2004)
Outgrow (2006)
Made in 20 (2007)
The Face (2008)
Identity (2010)

ENGLISH ALBUM
BoA (2009)

FAN CLUBS Jumping BoA (Korea), Soul (Japan)
OFFICIAL COLOR Yellow

---

giant Avex Entertainment, BoA's debut became a million copy seller and a major hit. *Listen to My Heart*, released in 2002, was the first album by a Korean to make its debut at the top of the Oricon album chart, and *Valenti*, in 2003, was even bigger.

For the next few years, BoA released hit after hit, alternating between Japan and Korea and Japanese and Korean albums.

Having firmly proven to be one of the biggest stars in Asia, BoA next set her sights on the West. She studied hard and put together her

If a single singer could represent K-pop, it would probably be BoA, one of Korea's greatest icons.

BoA has been the
biggest K-pop star in
Japan for more than
a decade.

first all-English album, led by a big push for the song "Eat You Up."

BoA's attempt to break into the American market in 2009 attracted plenty of attention, even if the conservative nature of mainstream media did not know what to make of her. But thanks to YouTube and other online music services, today the Western media realizes there are many different ways of measuring stardom.

And BoA keeps challenging herself. She was a judge on the popular Korean music program *K-Pop Star*, and more recently she has been trying her hand at acting. The year 2013 saw BoA's successful acting debut in the Korean TV drama *Expect Romance*, as well as her first starring role in a Hollywood dance film, *Make Your Move*. Thanks to the continuing rise of K-pop, maybe this will be the right time for BoA to find her way into the hearts and minds of global audiences.

BoA was discovered almost by accident when the SM Entertainment founder saw her and liked her smile.

JAY PARK

Sidus HQ

The story of Jay Park's rise to fame is one of the more unusual ones in K-pop, rising, falling terribly, only to rise again even more spectacularly, although the truth is, in many ways it is barely K-pop at all.

Jay Park started out as a typical teenager in Seattle, albeit a very talented one, listening to hip-hop and teaching himself how to b-boy dance and rap. It was Jay's mother who encouraged him to audition with JYP Entertainment. Jay excelled, and in early 2005 he was brought to Korea to begin the rigorous training program. In addition to the usual gauntlet of idol training, Jay also had to work on his Korean, which was pretty basic at the time. It was a tough, lonely time for Jay, but the hard work paid off, and in 2008 he made his debut with the group 2PM.

Right away, 2PM was one of the hottest boy groups in K-pop, reeling off a string of hits and lighting the Internet on fire. The sky was the limit, or so it seemed.

Unfortunately, just as Jay's career was taking off, someone unearthed some comments he had made online soon after coming to Korea, when he was lonely and having a tough time adjusting. They

FULL NAME
Park Jae-beom (박재범) April 25, 1987

KOREAN ALBUMS
New Breed (2012)
Tktk (2013)

KOREAN MINI-ALBUMS
Count on Me (Nothin' on You) (2010)
Take a Deeper Look (2011)
New Breed, Part 1 (2011)

FAN CLUBS Jay Effect, Jay Walkers

Bold, confident and creative, Jay Park is the leader of a new generation of K-pop stars.

Jay Park has an edgy side that sets him apart from a lot of K-pop.

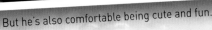

But he's also comfortable being cute and fun.

were not anything unusual for a frustrated teenager, but still they struck a chord with the public, and soon the public outrage built. Despite Jay's many fans, he was forced to leave the group and JYP Entertainment in 2010. His young career seemingly over, Jay returned to the United States while 2PM continued recording its new album without him.

Once again, the Internet would come to the rescue. In March 2010, Jay started a YouTube channel, where he posted a video of himself singing BoB's "Nothin' on You." In less than a day, that video landed two million views. Just like that, Jay got his career back.

This time, however, Jay was going to do it his own way. He started writing his own music, still plenty of melodious pop but also harder hip-hop and edgy dance tracks. On June 18, he returned to Korea where 1,000 fans were waiting for him at the airport. He released a three-song mini-album in July, and even though he wasn't on a major music label any more (he signed with Sidus HQ, a group better known for its big roster of acting talent), it quickly hit No. 1 on the charts.

A skilled rapper and composer, Jay Park is not just a K-pop star, he's simply a global star.

Jay has also turned out to be a good actor and performer. He did several guest spots on the Korean edition of *Saturday Night Live*, and in season 4 he actually joined the cast of the show.

Today, Jay is a rising star, with one foot in K-pop and the other in Western hip-hip and pop. He sports plenty of attitude and tattoos, far beyond what most of K-pop is comfortable with, but he also performed H.O.T's classic hit (and ultra cute song) "Candy" with H.O.T member Moon Hee-joon for a popular Korean variety show. Western producers who have spent time with Jay in the studio are all impressed by his vision and abilities.

How ironic is it that Korea's top crossover K-pop stars in 2013 would be Psy and Jay? The two men could not look any more different—Jay all abs and tattoos, Psy, er, not so much—but both are stars between two worlds, bringing a different element to K-pop while also bringing K-pop to the rest of the world.

RAIN

Rainy Entertainment, Cube Entertainment

Rain has not only spent much of the past ten years as perhaps the biggest solo star in K-pop, he was also the first K-pop star to make a significant impact in the West, although that impact wasn't so much for his music as his acting. Rain had a role in the big-budget *Speed Racer* and then starred in the gory action film *Ninja Assassin*.

Most importantly, he had a "feud" with TV talk show host and comedian Stephen Colbert. When Rain beat Colbert on a *Time* magazine Internet poll for top international celebrity, Colbert declared mock war on Rain, which only ended after Rain came on *The Colbert Report* and beat Stephen in a dance-off.

Rain grew up in a poor family in the western side of Seoul, in a neighborhood surrounded by universities. But Rain's dream wasn't to be a scholar, it was to dance. All the while he was growing up, Rain danced incessantly, practicing his moves with friends at various practice rooms in his neighborhood.

His first attempt at joining a K-pop group, Fan Club, was short-lived and not terribly memorable. When the group disbanded in 1999, Rain just kept dancing and auditioning for different music labels.

FULL NAME
Jung Ji-hoon [정지훈] June 25, 1982

KOREAN ALBUMS
Bad Guy (2002)
How to Avoid the Sun (2003)
It's Raining (2004)
Rain's World (2006)
Rainism (2008)

KOREAN MINI-ALBUM
Back to the Basic (2010)

JAPANESE ALBUMS
Eternal Rain (2006)
Rainism (2008)

JAPANESE MINI-ALBUM
Back to the Basics (2012)

FAN CLUB Clouds
OFFICIAL COLOR Silver

He's suave, he's dynamic, he's Rain.

Having just finished
his military service,
Rain is ready to thrill
fans like never before.

wasn't long before the company realized they had something special, and in 2002 Rain released his first album, *Bad Guy*.

Even then, he wasn't an instant superstar. It wasn't until his third album, released around the same time he starred in *Full House*, a TV drama that became incredibly popular all over Asia, that Rain took the leap to super stardom.

With his fifth album, Rain left JYP Entertainment and created his own record label. It was a tough period for him, but he still wrote most of the songs on his album and toured all over Asia and America—and acted in two Hollywood movies!

In July 2013, Rain completed his military service, and soon after signed up with Cube Entertainment. Everyone is waiting to see what Rain has in store for the next phase of his career.

Sadly, Rain's mother died before his first album came out. But even after all these years, he clearly still carries her in his heart. When he was released from military service, the first thing he did was drive to the cemetery where his mother's remains are kept to pay respects to her. Even though hundreds of fans were waiting for him at the gates of the military camp, Rain's thoughts were with his mother. Despite all the accolades and hits and movies, in many ways Rain is the most introverted of K-pop stars.

Despite oozing talent, he just wasn't able to convince anyone he had what it takes.

Until, one fateful day in 2000, he scored an audition with Park Jin-young. Park recognized something about Rain. "Tiger eyes," he said. He forced Rain to dance and audition for hours,

pushing him relentlessly. But when it was all over, Rain had a home at JYP Entertainment.

For the next two years, the training was tough, as it is for everyone in K-pop, but the thing is, Rain excelled. Each month, when JYP Entertainment made its talent evaluations, Rain kept winning. It

YOON MI-RAE

Feel Ghood Music

Over the past twenty years of K-pop, there has not been a performer as talented as Yoon Mi-rae, aka Tasha. K-pop employs a lot of rapping, but most of it is a uniquely Korean style. Tasha, however, raps as fiercely and sharply as anything out of New York City, with a boom like MC Lyte and the musicality of Monie Love. She is also a great singer, with a powerful, soulful voice that can handle a wide range of music.

Born in Texas, Tasha came to Korea as a teenager and started putting together a group. Eventually, Uptown would make its debut in 1997 and put out several albums, but a drug scandal led to the group's break-up in 2000.

Tasha was clearly the group's stand-out member and soon launched a solo career. Although never in the upper echelons of K-pop, Tasha was always deeply respected, whether recording more R&B/soul or full-out hip-hop.

Unfortunately, after a couple of albums, Tasha had some major problems with her record label and it would take years before she could free herself and record again. But when she did, it was probably her most important album, *T3—Yoon Mi Rae*.

For the first time, *T3—Yoon Mi Rae*, featured both her English initial and her Korean name and the album was Tasha's most personal. Most notable was the song "Black Happiness," a painfully honest reflection of what it was like growing up half-Korean and half-black in a society that often did not respect mixed-race couples and their children. She sang about being pointed at and whispered about, about hating the color of her skin and how music was often the only way to transcend her troubles.

Tasha had been dating the godfather of Korean hip-hop, Tiger JK, co-founder of Drunken Tiger, for many years. Then, in 2007,

Yoon Mi-rae, aka Tasha, has one of the best voices in all of Korean music.

they got married and soon had a son, Jordon, perhaps laying the groundwork for the next generation of Korean superstars.

Since then, Tasha has recorded several singles and done some great tours, as well as hosted the audition-survival show *Superstar K*. Too on the "real" hip-hop side to be fully K-pop, Tasha has never abandoned that side of her persona. Together with her husband and label mate Bizzy, the three formed a dance-music group MFBTY in 2012, with a wonderful song "Sweet Dream." It was never a big hit, but it served as a solid reminder that you never should get too hung up on genre. Artists like Yoon Mi-rae and her husband are always bigger than any label.

NAMES
Yoon Mi-rae; Tara Reid; T; Tasha
May 31, 1981

Former member of Uptown, Tashannie
Also member of MFBTY

ALBUMS
As Time Goes By (2001)
Gemini (2002)
To My Love (2002)
T Best (2003)
T3—Yoon Mi Rae (2007)

A great rapper and singer, Yoon Mi-rae is married to one of the first Korean rappers, Tiger JK.

IU is considered the little sister of the Korean entertainment industry.

IU
Last Fantasy 2

FULL NAME
Lee Ji-eun (이지은) May 16, 1993

KOREAN ALBUMS
Growing Up (2009)
Last Fantasy (2011)

KOREAN MINI-ALBUMS
Lost and Found (2008)
IU ... IM (2009)
Real (2010)

JAPANESE ALBUMS
I.U (2012)
Can You Hear Me? (2013)

FAN CLUB U-Ana (unofficial)
OFFICIAL COLOR n/a

IU

Loen Entertainment

At first, IU was a big failure in the Korean music industry. As a young adolescent she auditioned around twenty times for many music labels, never getting that lucky break. At long last, Loen saw something in the cute young singer and decided to take a chance. They wouldn't regret it.

Making her debut at just fifteen years old, after only a year in training, IU's first single and mini-album in 2008 did not make much of an impression on the charts; IU said it "failed horribly." But she was growing as an artist and kept working, and by the time her first full album came out the next year, IU was clearly a hot new talent to be reckoned with. With "Boo," IU and her company went with a cuter look, and considering how young she was, it was a good match for her style.

Since then, IU has gone from hit to hit, with light-hearted, infectious songs like "You & I" and "Good Day." Her second album, Last Fantasy, released in late 2011, did especially well, lighting up the charts. It's probably no coincidence that with Last Fantasy, IU was getting increasingly involved in her own songwriting.

In 2012, and just nineteen, IU had her first concert in Japan and also released a Japanese-language album, helping to spread her popularity overseas. Now twenty years old, IU is already releasing her third album. Already, though, the young teenager has grown into a mature young woman, with songs and a style reflecting those changes. While IU has joked before about getting married and settling down, it's clear that the beautiful young singer will be a major force in K-pop for as long as she wants to be.

IU is just twenty years old but already has three albums to her name.

CHAPTER 6

K-POP'S FUTURE

ROY KIM

After nearly twenty years, K-pop has shown its ability to endure, constantly evolving to absorb new music forms and trends. And with more K-pop bands than ever coming out of Korea's music labels, big and small, there's no doubt that K-pop will endure for years to come. No one knows the future, but here are some up-and-coming bands that have the potential to become the next Big Bang or Shinhwa.

One pattern is clear in this list—the importance that *American Idol*-style television audition shows now have in Korea. But you should know that talent shows are not really new in Korea. Back in the late 1970s, they were all the rage as Korea's biggest TV stations showcased talented young people, turning them into stars. One thing is for sure, though, as long as K-pop continues to thrive, there is going to be no shortage of contenders.

HISTORY

History A five-man group introduced by Loen Entertainment in 2013. With a Queen-like vocal-and-piano intro, History's "Dreamer" shows that History could be more than just another boy band. It could have the diversity to push K-pop's boundaries.

VIXX A six-man group signed to Jellyfish Entertainment. VIXX turned a lot of heads with its rather gothic and mysterious "Hyde" in 2013. Group leader N made a comment online about not wanting to become an idol, which confused a lot of fans about what he's doing in a K-pop group.

BOYS REPUBLIC

Boys Republic In another sign of how K-pop is growing internationally, Boys Republic is a group put together by Universal Music Korea. The five-member group, launched in June 2013, has already made quite a splash, thanks in part to Universal teaming up Boys Republic with some of the most talented producers in K-pop.

Wonder Boyz A four-man group led by talented rapper Bak Chi Gi. The group's single "Tarzan" featured a reggaeton sound that's pretty unusual in K-pop. The question is, how will they harness their talents to find a niche in the crowded pop music market?

Lee Hi Lee Hi finished second in the first season of *K-Pop Star*, but for YG Entertainment she was their winner. Just seventeen years old (she was born in 1996), Lee is one of the youngest stars in K-pop, but she made a strong professional debut in late 2012, winning Best Rookie awards from several leading award shows.

15& This duo features Park Ji-min, the winning of *K-Pop Star* season 1, and Baek Ye-rin, who has been training with JYP Entertainment since she was just ten years old. Together, they made their debut in 2012 when they were both fifteen, hence the group's name.

15&

Akdong Musicians A young brother/sister team who lived for many years in Mongolia, Akdong Musicians has quickly become a favorite in Korea, thanks to winning *K-Pop Star* season 2. More like Busker Busker than "pure" K-pop, the duo's unique style is a sign of how Korean popular music is broadening and becoming more varied these days. Their songs are undeniably fun and witty, such as the very cute "Don't Cross Your Legs."

Roy Kim The winner of *Superstar K4*, Roy is one of the fastest rising stars in Korean pop music, with a sound that is more folksy and organic than typical K-pop. He

ROY KIM

has only released a couple of singles since his 2012 TV win, but the sky is the limit for this young singer.

Crayon Pop This five-woman group made a quiet debut in 2012, but thanks to an unusual, low-budget video for "Bar Bar Bar" that went viral in 2013, it is suddenly one of the hottest groups around.

The video features the girls in bright but basic clothing, and all wearing safety helmets as they bounce and perform ridiculously simple dance moves. The odd look caught on, causing the song to slowly climb the charts all the way to No. 1. The group was even invited to perform at Korea's version of the Global Gathering electronic music festival.

Traveling to Korea

A few years ago, traveling to Korea, especially Seoul, could be a bit daunting. Signs were lacking, hotels expensive and communication difficult. But even as Korean culture has grown more popular abroad over the last decade, Korea has become a more inviting, friendly country for visitors.

Today, there are plenty of resources to help out tourists, making exploring Korea more fun and interesting than ever. There are walking tours and shopping tours, and most of the big ticketing websites have English (and other) options, helping you buy tickets to concerts, musicals or whatever else you might want to try. Interpark is one of the best (ticket.interpark.com/global).

Of course, finding a place to stay is one of the most important parts of any vacation. Once upon a time, hotels could be difficult if you weren't a total moneybags. Mid-range hotels were tough to come by. Today, however, the options really have multiplied.

Guesthouses and B&Bs have sprung up all over Seoul, many of them in the best parts of town, especially in Hongdae, operated by friendly people who like playing host to international guests.

Yellow Submarine (yellow-submarine.kr) in Yeonnam-dong, a short walk from Hongdae, is one popular option.

Kpop Stay (kpopstay.com) gets great marks from many budget travelers and is right in the middle of Hongdae, so you cannot beat the location.

Cozzzy (cozzzy.co.kr) is another good option for the Hongdae area.

For other parts of town, in the Hyehwa area, another fun, student neighborhood famous for its theaters, you can stay at **Stay in GAM** (facebook.com/Stayingam).

In Insa-dong, a charming part of town close to the old palaces, **Banana Backpackers** (bananabackpackers.com) is popular.

On the slopes of Mount Namsan in the heart of town, there are many guesthouses, including **Soo Guest-house** (sooguesthouse.com) and **Bong House** (www.bonghouse.net).

South of the river, in expensive parts of town like Apgujeong and Gangnam, guesthouses are unsurprisingly much harder to find. But for people who have a bit more money, Seoul also is starting to get into the boutique hotel trend, with more creative and fun options springing up around town. Two of the most popular options are the **Hotel the Designers** (thedesignershotel.com), with one location in Samseong-dong, in the rich, southeast of the city, and another in Hongdae, the cool bar and artsy part of Seoul in the west. Each room was created by a different designer and the results can be pretty funky.

If you want to stay in the fashionable Garosu-gil neighborhood, then **La Casa** (hotellacasa.kr) is probably your best bet.

For a really different experience, there is always the **Rakkojae** (www.rkj.co.kr) guesthouse, a beautiful *hanok* (traditional building) in the center of old Seoul. This *hanok* is more than 130 years old, but the interiors are gorgeous, giving you a taste of what life used to be like in olden-day Korea, well, the olden days for rich people, anyhow.

Remember that Korea gets pretty hot in the summer (and hot and wet in mid-July) and pretty cold in the winter, so whenever you choose to come, be prepared and dress appropriately.

These days, most of the banks in Korea are much more international than they used to be, so it is not too hard to find ATMs that work with banks cards from all over the world accepted. A lot of ATMs stop operating after midnight, so be careful about that. Convenience store ATMs usually run 24-hours, although they can be a bit dodgy.

Taxis are relatively cheap in Seoul and are often a good way to get around quickly. But if you choose to try out the public transportation system, it is quite well developed, if a little disorienting at first. Seoul now has nine subway lines and several other train lines that work with the subway (www.smrt.co.kr/).

Buses and subways cost a flat 1,100 *won* for your average ride, although longer trips cost more. Everything is electronic now, so if you plan on taking public transportation, the first thing you'll need to do is get a T-Money card and charge it up with some money. Fortunately, the T-Money machines are multilingual, ubiquitous and fairly easy to use.

Restaurants can be a bit intimidating because most menus are in Korean, but English and other language menus are increasingly common (mostly Japanese and Chinese), especially in the more tourist-friendly parts of town.

Remember that nearly everywhere in Seoul there is no shortage of 24-hour convenience stores, so if you need water or toiletries or whatever at three in the morning, you should be in luck.

Acknowledgements

A huge thanks to all the music companies and their international PR teams who participated in this book: SM Entertainment, JYP Entertainment, YG Entertainment, TS Entertainment, Star Empire Entertainment, Starship, Pledis, Loen, Cube Entertainment, Jungle Entertainment, Sidus HQ, FNC, CJ E&M, Nega Networks and Big Hit.

I am also incredibly grateful to everyone who was willing to be interviewed for this book, in particular Brian Joo, Kevin Kim and Simon and Martina Stawski.

Thanks to Robert Koehler for his excellent photos of Seoul, as well as all the other individuals and companies who supplied photos for the book.

And thanks to all of *you* who bought this book. K-pop producers in Korea may be big companies with a lot of marketing power, but the success of K-pop around the world has very much been a grassroots sensation, powered by people like you who found out about it online or by word of mouth. It's pretty awesome to be a part of your network.

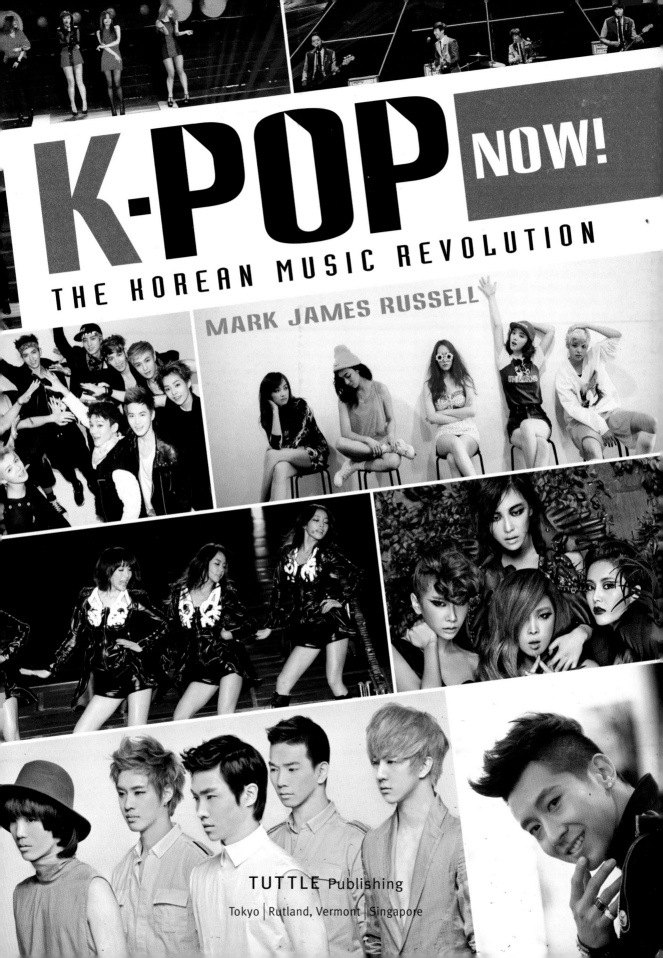

K-POP NOW!

THE KOREAN MUSIC REVOLUTION

MARK JAMES RUSSELL

TUTTLE Publishing

Tokyo | Rutland, Vermont | Singapore

CONTENTS

K-pop fans can never get enough of their favorite groups.

When B.A.P. takes the stage, you know something special is going to happen.

Introduction
THE STATE OF K-POP

Wonder Girls is one of the most successful K-pop groups of the last few years.

The stadium lights darken, replaced by thousands of fluorescent sticks waving madly as screams fill the air.

Then comes the boom and flash of fireworks from the stage as silhouettes strike dramatic poses, waiting to begin. Somehow, the impossibly loud screaming grows louder.

Finally, as anticipation reaches an apex, a deep bass kicks in. The stage lights suddenly blast, the bodies on stage start dancing. The concert has begun, and for the next two hours the cries of joy from the legions of fans will not stop.

It's K-pop (an abbreviation for Korean pop), the musical mania that has come out of South Korea and enraptured a world of fans. More than just music, K-pop is also about fashion and style, fun and the future, of a new wave of attitude coming from an old world. And, of course, it is also about the beautiful stars and their adoring fans.

The names of the bands may look strange—Big Bang, Super Junior, 2PM, 2NE1, TVXQ!, Girls' Generation, U-Kiss, T-ara, EXO, JYJ, 4Minute, MBLAQ. And as K-pop becomes more popular, the list grows ever longer.

For me, it's hard to believe K-pop has come so far. When I first arrived in Korea, one of the first and greatest K-pop groups, H.O.T, was just getting started, setting off

a wave of mania that could not compare to anything I had seen in North America or Europe. Their first big hit, "Candy," was on the air and on TV everywhere, and at the time H.O.T featured a cuddly, cute image, with the group's five members dressed in bright colors, often in large, plush jumpsuits. Only later would they take a turn toward the goth. But soon came other groups, nearly as popular—S.E.S., FinKL, g.o.d., Shinhwa and more.

I soon began writing about Korean music for a variety of Western publications, including *Billboard*, talking about the coolest new groups and the hottest new music labels. And gradually it became clear that K-pop was also

building followings outside of Korea, in other parts of Asia. But the question I was asked by people in the Korean music business, over and over again, was "When will Korea have a Destiny's Child?" Or, later, a Beyonce or a Justin Timberlake? That is, when would a K-pop group become big in the United States?

At the time, the question seemed ridiculous. K-pop was catchy but it was so far away from the big pop stars of America. When I posed that question to Western music executives, they would also answer the same way: "Why would we want a Korean Destiny's Child when we already have Destiny's Child? We already have Beyonce

and Justin Timberlake, too." K-pop would have to wait.

The thing is, K-pop didn't want to wait. It kept growing and pushing, winning over more and more fans. And then came Psy and "Gangnam Style." Goofy Park Jae-sang, who had been singing and dancing for a decade with his catchy, silly songs. But "Gangnam Style" was even goofier and catchier than usual, and this time the West got the joke. Leading websites and celebrities started tweeting and linking to the "Gangnam Style" video on YouTube and soon the song took off. And somehow, it kept getting bigger and bigger, until today it tops *1.8 billion* views, nearly twice as many as the next biggest song.

Even before Psy, K-pop had been growing. It spent much of the 2000s spreading around Asia, with BoA becoming a major star in Japan, and Rain finding huge popularity around the region. But, like a lot of people, I thought it was mostly a local trend. However, as I spent time on the Internet, reading the popular Internet forums, I couldn't help but notice other names beginning to appear, people from other locations around the world.

The first time I heard K-pop in Europe was in 2009, in a dingy local café on the western end of Barcelona, far from the tourist strip. It was a quiet Sunday morning, and I was enjoying a coffee and a snack when I suddenly noticed a strangely familiar sound on the radio. The music was bright and poppy, in different chords than Spanish pop usually uses. Then I finally heard the voices. They were singing in Korean. I asked the bartender, a middle-aged Catalan man, how he could have K-pop on his stereo and he shrugged and said he just liked it. No big deal.

Soon after that, K-pop began springing up everywhere. SM Entertainment held two hugely popular shows in Paris in 2011. The group JYJ had concerts in Barcelona and Frankfurt. Girls' Generation appeared on David Letterman and other US television shows. Groups like Big Bang and Super Junior started playing in Europe, the United States and South America. Clearly, something was going on.

There are also more groups than ever, with dozens now making their

It's amazing, but in just five years 2PM has become one of the leading groups in K-pop.